Supervision
of the
Sex Offender

Georgia Cumming & Maureen Buell

Safer Society Press

Design: Whitman Communications Group
Editor: Alice Fins, Publications Managing Editor
          American Correctional Association

ISBN: 1–884444–40–7

$25.00

The Safer Society Press
P.O. Box 340
Brandon, VT 04733
(802) 247-3132

SaferSocietyPress

Table of Contents

Foreword

The Safer Society Press, a division of the Safer Society Foundation, Inc., is proud to present *The Supervision of the Sex Offender*. It is unique in providing a practical, detailed guide on effectively supervising sex offenders in the community. Authors Georgia Cumming and Maureen Buell have drawn on their more than 40 years of work in probation and parole to refute the conventional wisdom that "Nothing works." They have seen in Vermont that when carefully and thoroughly assessed, many sex offenders *can* be treated and effectively and safely supervised in the community as an alternative to incarceration or upon release from a correctional facility.

Supervision of the Sex Offender describes techniques and methods to help corrections staff and treatment providers determine whether a sex offender is appropriate for probation and community treatment or requires incarceration with possible later parole, supervision and treatment. Cumming and Buell outline pre-sentence investigations, briefly review theories of offending and typologies of offenders, describe risk assessment and treatment, and discuss the controversial issues of confidentiality and public disclosure. Recognizing that community safety is of paramount concern, they describe ways that a supervision network involving members of the offender's community can help an offender abstain from abuse, effectively promoting community safety. Further, they identify typical cues to help probation supervisors recognize when an offender is continuing sexually abusive behavior.

Avoiding jargon, Cumming and Buell illustrate their major points with examples drawn from their experiences, making this manual illuminating for corrections and criminal justice personnel—including probation/parole officers, judges, prosecutors, and police officers—as well as for social workers, victim advocates, and therapists. *Supervision of the Sex Offender* is also a practical and useful book for family and friends of sex offenders and for others whose lives interact with theirs.

Supervision of the Sex Offender combines information from the fields of sexual abuse prevention and treatment and corrections in a valuable resource for your personal or professional library.

Robert E. Freeman-Longo, MRC, LPC, CCJS
Director, Safer Society Press

Introduction

In the late 1970s, Vermont found itself in a position similiar to many other states: the number of incarcerated sex offenders was increasing as was the number of sex offenders under community supervision. A task force was established to study and develop a statewide sex-offender treatment program. The task force's final report recommended a two-pronged approach: a treatment program for offenders while they were incarcerated and a community-based program for those considered lower risk and amenable to community treatment. The community-based program also would continue the treatment of the incarcerated offender upon his release onto parole.

Using cognitive-behavioral techniques in conjunction with the Relapse Prevention Model, the Vermont Treatment Program for Sexual Aggressors (VTPSA) was established in 1982. In 1983, the first outpatient group for treating sex offenders began. Since then, the treatment program for incarcerated sex offenders has quadrupled, and community-based treatment groups exist throughout the state.

As a small state, Vermont provided an ideal environment to pilot a systems approach to the treatment and supervision of the sex offender. Probation, parole, and institutions are under the umbrella of the Department of Corrections, which makes continuity of supervision possible. Additionally, specialized sex offender training, sponsored by the Department of Corrections, was provided to judges, prosecutors, social workers, police officers, victim advocates, and therapists. Through our years of training and consulting in other states, we have learned that this approach can be used successfully even in larger and more diverse states than ours. For example, in a large state, it could be applied county by county.

This handbook parallels the sequential movement of the offender through the criminal justice system, beginning at the time of conviction. Chapter 1 on "Presentence Investigations" discusses the information needed to determine offenders' amenability to treatment and to evaluate their risk to the community. This is an important chapter, even for those officers not involved in the writing of presentence reports, as it addresses the interview techniques for exploring offense history. Chapters 2 and 3 discuss supervision issues, and Chapter 4 outlines the uses of the plethysmograph, the polygraph, and psychopharmacology in the assessment and/or supervision of sex offenders. Chapter 5 provides a basic introduction to who the sex offender is and a sex-offender typology. This chapter also looks at the effectiveness of treatment and the overall cost of providing treatment to this population. Chapters 6 and 7 address treatment issues particular to sex offenders, and Chapters 8 and 9 address special populations within sex offenders. Chapter 10 outlines the working relationships among various agencies when a systems approach is used. The addendum includes a glossary of technical terms and a sample of forms used in Vermont that may be useful in other jurisdictions.

The philosophy and techniques described in this work have evolved from our combined forty-year work experience as probation and parole officers, as managers, and as program coordinators for sex-offender treatment programs. Our supervision strategy has a philosophical base:

- The majority of sex offenders can learn how to manage and control their sexually deviant behaviors.
- Mandated specialized treatment as part of probation or parole conditions is essential and effective.
- Not all sex offenders are amenable to treatment; those who are not should be screened out of community-based treatment programs.
- Sex offenders have a responsibility to stop their abusive behaviors; if they choose not to, they should be incarcerated.
- Providing treatment to sex offenders reduces future victimization and is prevention.

While sex offenders should be held accountable for their crimes, those who work with them must be humane and respectful. This in no way implies coddling the offender or excusing abusive behaviors. We believe that effective behavior change occurs in an atmosphere that acknowledges and supports the offenders' potential for change, thereby reducing the threat they pose to their families and communities.

The purpose for writing this manual was to provide probation and parole officers with concrete strategies in their supervision of sex offenders. However, other professionals involved with sex offenders, as well as family members of the offender, will find this book helpful in understanding what exactly goes on in the supervision of sex offenders. It is important that those working with or befriending the sex offender be familiar with the role and functions of the probation/parole officer. Thus, the information in this book should be helpful for people in the court system, those who work with community corrections, mental health providers, social workers, and a range of others whose personal or professional life includes the sex offender.

Chapter 1

Presentence Investigation Report

The presentence investigation is a report ordered by the judge after an offender has been found guilty by a jury or a judge or has entered a plea of guilty or *nolo contendere* to the presenting charge/s. The district attorney or the defense attorney also may recommend to the judge that a presentence report be ordered. The purpose of this report is to provide information about the defendant to the court to assist in the disposition of the case. This report is generally prepared by the probation department.

In the presentence report, the probation officer includes detailed information about the defendant's offense of record, criminal record, family and personal history, employment and financial history, substance abuse history, and prior periods of community supervision and/or incarceration. At the conclusion of the report, the probation officer assesses this information and makes a recommendation to the court as to disposition.

Assessing the needs and risks of the sex offender prior to the commencement of supervision is a critical function for the probation officer. The ideal time for this assessment is during the writing of a presentence investigation report. Although presentence reports are not always ordered on sex offenders, the presentence investigation report is an ideal format for discussing this assessment. The following sections have been organized and highlighted for easy reference for those probation officers doing a general intake or for parole officers who are developing an initial case plan for a parolee who is or has been a sex offender.

With a presentence report on a sex offender, it is important to be alert to behavioral and attitudinal traits that prevent honesty or, at best, full disclosure. Some sex offenders are in total denial about their abusive behavior, and they prove unwilling to recognize and give up the denial. If this remains the case, they cannot be treated successfully and should be denied access to community-based treatment. For them, incarceration is the appropriate disposition. Some sex offenders pretend to want treatment but choose not to meaningfully engage in the treatment process once they are placed in community treatment. Of course, there are sex offenders who are amenable to treatment but who pose such a high risk to the community that their treatment initially must occur within an incarcerated setting.

How then can a probation officer make a responsible recommendation regarding the following: amenability to treatment, risk factors posed by offenders to their victims and the community, and the special conditions of probation that are tailored to the offenders' precursors to deviant behavior. It is not the purpose of this chapter to discuss the punitive consequences of committing a sexual offense, nor will it address the different sentencing guidelines in various states that may restrict the probation officer from making certain types of recommendations. Instead, this chapter will address what type of information the probation officer needs to determine amenability to treatment and to evaluate risk to the community and how this information is gathered.

Because many sex offenders present a socially acceptable facade, the chaos in their lives is not readily apparent to the probation officer who may be used to dealing with a more overtly criminal client. Many sex offenders, for example, have stable employment, a social support group of either family or friends, and no criminal record. They score low on correctional risk assessment instruments, but, in reality, present a high risk to the community. As the generic risk assessment instruments used by many probation departments will not accurately assess a sex offender's risk to the community, a traditional presentence investigation does not address the essential issues needed to determine the sex offender's risk and treatment amenability. For example, an in-depth sexual history must go beyond the details of the offense of record. A presentence investigation report on sex offenders should include the following: the summary of all pertinent documents, detailed offense statements, a personal and sexual history of the offenders, evaluation of the offenders' amenability to specialized treatment, and their risk to their potential victims and the community.

Sex offenders often lead elaborately secret lives, and they often deny or minimize their sexually deviant patterns and their crimes. Although many sex offenders are treatable, they are not appropriate for treatment if they remain in denial about their sexually abusive behaviors. Because of this, a central focus throughout the interview process of the presentence investigation will be to break through the denial and the deceit. It should be noted that completing a comprehensive presentence investigation report on a sex offender takes more time than a traditional presentence report and requires development of additional interview and investigative skills. In assigning caseloads, probation supervisors should be aware of this fact and accordingly adjust caseload requirements.

Document Review

Taking the time to review all documents is essential and should occur before the first interview with the sex offender. This enables the probation officer to learn aspects of the sex offender's history that the offender may choose to omit or gloss over during the interview. This enables the probation officers also to strategize in advance if they are aware of how the sex offenders may deny or rationalize their behaviors. However, not all information will be immediately available, such as out-of-state record checks, and with the time limit on many presentence reports, the interview will need to begin without them.

Reviewing the police affidavit is mandatory, as is speaking with the investigating officer for information that may have come to light after the affidavit was written. For example, there may be an ongoing investigation involving victims in another county. Also, read the victim's statement because often it is the only eye-witness account.

If the sex offender's statement is available, read it; look for a pattern of denial. If denial is present, watch for the use of alibis, or the admission of guilt. Notice, as well, the offender's attitude toward his victims.

Many sex offenders do not have extensive criminal records, but for those offenders who do, it is important to obtain affidavits on those prior convictions. It is not uncommon, for example, for a simple assault to have been reduced from an attempted sexual assault, or perhaps the burglary was an attempted rape in which the offender was scared off by the return of a roommate. In the writing of the presentence investigation report, each conviction should include a short summary of the offense. This documentation begins to record the risks and patterns of deviant behavior. It also may show an escalation of behavior prior to the current offense.

If the offender has lived in other states, a record check should be obtained from those states. A record check from the National Crime Information Center (NCIC) should be done routinely, although not all convictions will show on an NCIC report. If a collateral contact indicates legal difficulties in another state and the record check fails to show a conviction, it is important to follow up with phone calls to that state. The NCIC report is dependent upon good data entry, and it will not be 100 percent reliable. On occasion, you will uncover a conviction which did not show up on the record check.

A psychosexual report may have been completed prior to the presentence investigation. These reports can be extremely helpful to the probation officer, especially if the therapist completing the report has expertise evaluating sex offenders. As long as these reports are a part of the district attorney's file, there should be no problem as to access. If the offender needs to sign release of information forms for you to obtain this record, do this at the beginning of the first interview with the offender.

If the offender has been under previous supervision, review these records for past behavior and attitude under supervision. If the offender was in treatment, the therapist and the previous probation officer should be interviewed, if not before the first interview with the offender, certainly before the second interview.

Offender History

A thorough interview with the offender is as important as being familiar with all the previously mentioned documents. It is a lengthy process composed of equally important components. If possible, two separate interviews with the offender should take place. The time between the interviews will provide the opportunity to interview collateral contacts and verify information the offender provides. The collateral contacts should be reliable, trustworthy, and able to withstand legal scrutiny.

It is essential the probation officer be in control of the interview. Sex offenders are used to exerting power, and controlling and manipulating their surroundings. For example, do not allow the offender to interrupt you, or to go off on tangents. Maintaining control of the interview does not mean abusing your authority as a probation officer; it does mean being assertive and direct in your questioning.

Personal History

Obtaining the offender's family and personal history should occur during the initial interview. This allows the probation officer to discuss areas that are typically non-threatening to the offender and provides an opportunity to gain rapport with the offender before delving into the sexual aspects of the report, areas that are more threatening. Personal history interviews are familiar territory to probation officers; however, when interviewing a sex offender, explore certain areas in greater depth.

FAMILY: In the family history section, obtain the following: names, ages, and addresses of family members. Addresses should be requested at the beginning, not left until last, as offenders may not be as forthcoming at the end of the interview, particularly if they do not want a family member contacted. Find out which family members offenders maintain contact with, and which they avoid and why. Obtain a family history of criminal activity, substance abuse, physical and/or sexual abuse. If possible, contact the family members the offenders state they do not want contacted. Sometimes, you may uncover a history of physical or sexual abuse by the offenders by interviewing family members.

MARITAL/RELATIONSHIP: Relationship history should be obtained, including the ages and sex of the ex-partners' children. This data collection is essential, particularly if the offender is a first-time convicted child molester who on the surface appears to engage in age-appropriate relationships. For example, a presentence report was completed on a married man who had fondled the nine-year-old son of a neighbor. This man had no prior convictions. The probation officer interviewed one of his ex-wives and was told her three teenage daughters had been sexually abused by this man. She had reported it to social services, but no charges were brought after this offender moved to another state. Further incidences of sexual abuse are sometimes discovered this way, and probation officers are in a position that enables them to easily conduct these collateral interviews. Explore the possibility of physical abuse, particularly with rapists and incest offenders, where the issues of dominance and control may be exhibited in the family unit.

EMPLOYMENT: Many sex offenders present normal employment records. The problems other criminal offenders habitually have, such as lateness, absenteeism, conflicts with bosses or customers are not typical of many sex offenders. Nonetheless, it is vital to analyze all areas of the sex offender's employment, as scrutiny could reveal inappropriate work. For example, if the offender sexually abuses children, a job providing access to children, such as a fast food employee in a mall, is inappropriate. Other risks may include excessive work hours, sporadic absenteeism, and frequent job changes. Off-work contact with other employees who have children may need to be curtailed unless there is disclosure of the offender's crime.

These patterns, when identified, may reveal the potential for sexual abuse or indicate the difficulties the offender may present under supervision. Whether the investigation requires no more than interviews with employers or whether it requires time-consuming out-of-state employment checks, such probing is vital and often reveals essential information that otherwise would have gone undetected.

FINANCIAL: Financial history should include current debts and assets. Individuals' levels of stability are often reflected in how they manage their finances. Being heavily in debt or spending impulsively could impact on the financial responsibilities surrounding treatment costs. Addressing treatment costs at time of sentencing can prevent problems later on, particularly with offenders who use lack of money as the reason for dropping out of treatment.

MEDICAL: Medical history is particularly important with elderly or chronically ill offenders. Sex offenders may use their age or medical condition as a reason not to participate in treatment. Defense attorneys may argue that incarceration would be a death sentence for their client and therefore unreasonably harsh. An accurate evaluation from the offender's physician is important. Asking pointed questions may reveal multiple physicians and a misuse of medications.

MILITARY: Military records should be sent for even though the information may come weeks after the presentence deadline. Military records can be unrevealing, but at times they can be very informative. If nothing else, it is another way to evaluate the offender's level of honesty. Equally important is the offender's level of adjustment to the military. As military service is often the first time people leave the family home, they may engage in certain behaviors for the first time. As one young rapist described his enlistment, "It was my first time away from home, no one knew me. I could do anything I wanted." This individual, whose behaviors up to that time had involved peeping and exhibitionism, escalated rapidly to cruising for victims to rape. He was arrested for two rape attempts before being discharged from the service and returning home. Within weeks of returning home, he committed his first documented rape.

SUBSTANCE ABUSE: A complete drug and alcohol history should be taken and treatment records obtained, if the offender has been in a treatment program or participated in any type of outpatient counseling. A common response from sex offenders who admit to substance abuse problems is to blame alcohol as the sole cause of their sexually abusive behavior. Alcohol does not cause an offender to sexually abuse, although alcohol does reduce inhibitions. Sex offenders also use alcohol to access victims, as with the case with child molesters who always have beer in their refrigerator to offer the adolescents they invite over to their homes. It is essential for offenders to have their drug or alcohol problems under control for community treatment and supervision to be effective.

At the conclusion of the personal history portion of the interview, all releases of information should be obtained and signed. After the in-depth review of records, the interview of the offender and collateral interviews, a predatory child molester, previously undetected, can be uncovered.

Collateral Interviews

The collateral interviews with employers, family members, and friends may provide additional information about the offender, but more importantly they will provide the probation officer with the opportunity to evaluate the offender's level of honesty. Aside from the persons previously mentioned, it may be important to conduct the following interviews:

> **OFFENDER'S FAMILY/HOUSEMATES**—Interview the offender's housemates to determine the level of risk the offender's home may present. Questions to ask are as follows: Are they aware of the conviction? Do they believe the offender is guilty? Do they use alcohol or drugs? Will they agree to no longer bring alcohol into the home? Do they have children, relatives, or friends under the age of eighteen who frequent the house? Will they be a member of the supervision network? (see page 39)
>
> If the offender is living at home, a parent may be more enabling or misleading than an unrelated housemate. However, a parent may also be very helpful in

addressing the problems the offender may have with proper information. Be wary of automatically assuming that the parent of a sex offender will be enabling and not helpful.

The probation officer should determine where a sex offender is allowed to live. Depending upon your agency's general conditions of probation, a special condition giving the probation officer the authority to approve all residences is necessary.

EX-SPOUSE/EX-PARTNER—Interview ex-partners to determine the age and sex of their children when the offender was living in their home. Perhaps the offender's ex-partner had grandchildren or nieces and nephews who frequented their home. Assess whether the offender was physically, verbally, or emotionally violent toward individuals in the home.

CLERGY—Interview the religious/spiritual leader if the offender is a member of an organized religion. If time constraints prevent this during the presentence investigation, the supervising probation officer should do it. Some offenders have used the members of their church as an avenue for accessing potential victims. Other offenders change churches or rotate churches to avoid detection while keeping all their options to abuse open. Determining the extent of the disclosure the offender will need to make to church members will need to be assessed.

SUPPORT GROUPS SUCH AS ALCOHOLICS ANONYMOUS/NARCOTICS ANONYMOUS SPONSOR—After an arrest, some offenders "find" religion while other offenders "find" Alcoholics Anonymous or Narcotics Anonymous. One way to determine sincerity is whether the sex offender has acquired a sponsor and is working the step program. If the offender has an Alcoholics Anonymous/Narcotics Anonymous sponsor, he or she should be interviewed.

VICTIM—Most states require the probation officer to include a victim-impact statement in the presentence investigation report. Interviewing a victim to obtain an impact statement does not require asking questions about the abuse. If the probation officer has questions about the offense or is questioning the validity of the victim statement, the probation officer should seek clarification by interviewing the social services investigator, the police, or the district attorney regarding their concerns. Most victims have been interviewed numerous times, and the probation officer's job of evaluating risk to the community does not necessitate interviewing the victim about the abuse itself.

One of the goals of the interview should be to not further traumatize the victim. The following protocol is recommended in victim interviews:

Adult Victim: Check with the prosecutor before contacting the victim. It may be that the victim has written an impact statement for the prosecutor and wishes no further contact with the legal system. In that case, the victim would not be contacted.

When calling the victim, explain your role and the purpose of the impact statement. Emphasize that you will not be asking questions about the assault itself. Because rape victims have experienced powerlessness, it is important to give control of the interview over to the victim. This is partially accomplished by allowing the victim to decide when, where, how, and if the interview takes place.

Include both the financial and emotional impact of the sexual assault in the impact statement. If the victim was raped in her bedroom by an intruder, it may be that the victim had to sell all her bedroom furniture or is now afraid to live alone. Both these situations have a financial and an emotional impact and should be included in the statement.

Be prepared to answer questions about the legal proceedings and possible consequences to the offender. There is always the possibility the court may place a rapist on probation. Explore in advance what conditions of probation or parole would make the victim feel safer.

Child Victim: After contacting the district attorney, the next phone call would be to the social worker or the parent, depending on the circumstances of the offense. For example, with an incest offender, the social worker is contacted first. If the child is too young to interview or the social worker or parents recommend against it, then the parents and social worker would be interviewed for the impact statement. If the victim has a therapist, it is helpful to interview this person, especially in cases of incest. As with the adult victim, it is important to clarify that you will not be asking the child any questions about the abuse itself unless the victim chooses to discuss it.

Adolescents often want to be interviewed, and they may have many questions about the legal proceedings. If the case involves incest, it is best to interview the victim apart from the custodial parent although this will not be possible without the guardian's permission. Many probation officers do not have experience working with young children, and this interview may cause some discomfort which could be detected by the child. For those officers, it may be best to restrict their interview to the social worker, therapist, and/or appropriate caregiver.

Forms of Denial

To ensure an effective sentencing recommendation, it is vital that sex offenders disclose honestly and thoroughly their criminal offenses. To achieve this end, the probation officer must attempt to push through the denial, minimization, and rationalization that are usually encountered during the taking of the offense history. The anticipation of the sex offender's potential for resistance and denial is the probation officer's greatest ally in recognizing and dispensing with them.

The fact that sex offenses are illegal and entail social ostracism are two reasons that the sex offender denies and evades responsibility. Compounding these issues is that from the arrest to the involvement of the probation officer, considerable time has passed, during which offenders have had the opportunity to gather the support of family, friends, and employers, all of whom may want to believe their innocence. Suffice it to say, that these reasons enhance the probability that sex offenders will not be forthcoming.

Denial is not an either/or proposition. Denial can take many forms, and it is important to look at the different aspects of denial as this will assist probation officers in their interview strategy and in their final assessment.

1. **Denial of Responsibility**—The denial of responsibility can take two forms. One is physical denial. This occurs when offenders do not deny that the sexual abuse occurred, they simply state that they are not the perpetrator. They may offer an alibi as a way of proving their innocence. They may have parents or spouses who will collude with them and be part of the alibi.

The second is psychological denial. Offenders may deny the offense by saying that they are not that kind of person and therefore they could not have done it. Offenders may try to discredit the victims by calling the victims liars or vindictive. For example, the incest offender may talk about his daughter entering her adolescence and becoming rebellious against his rules. He may say he was only being a responsible parent who was enforcing discipline. He bemoans the fact that his daughter, over the last year, has begun to lie, stay out past curfew, and run away from home. He states the charges against him are his daughter's way of getting back at him.

2. **Denial of Intent**—In this incidence, offenders may admit some parts of the offense but deny that there was any intent on their part to commit the offense. The exhibitionist may insist he was just urinating and had no intent of exposing himself to others. One exhibitionist did acknowledge a problem, but when explored in more depth, the problem he identified was one of choosing the wrong places to urinate.

This type of denial may also take the form of the alcoholic blackout:

> I had been drinking heavily that day, I can't remember how I got home, I'm not saying A——- is lying. I just don't remember the evening. I do know that if I did what she says I did, I would never have done it sober.

Another example is the offender convicted of attempted sexual assault of a teenage boy who described his offense as simply a "wrestling match" which was misinterpreted. In this incident, the offender is saying that he did not intend to harm the victim; therefore, any harm that may have occurred is not his fault.

3. **Denial of Harm**—This occurs when offenders may admit aspects of the offense but deny victims were harmed. From the offenders' perspective, if the victims are not harmed, then what they did is not so serious. This may take the form of the incest offender saying his daughter now has a boyfriend, so what occurred between them could not have been that harmful.

Or, a sex offender may deny the harm of the assault itself, as the offender who raped his ex-girlfriend did: "I don't see what the problem is, it's not as if we never had sex before. It's not as if I hit her."

4. **Frequency**—The offender's statement of how many times the abuse occurred may be much less than what the victim says occurred. This is common with offenders who offend the same victim over a long period of time.

> I'm not going to say it didn't happen, but it didn't happen the way she says it did. I only had intercourse with her once, no way was it more than that. Maybe I would touch or rub her, but definitely not the intercourse.

The victim in this case stated the offender had sexually assaulted her every Saturday night for the last year.

5. **Intrusiveness**—Some offenders will admit some sexual acts and deny others. They may admit masturbating their victims and performing oral sex on them but will deny anally penetrating them.

6. **Denial of Fantasy**—Some offenders admit the abuse but deny any fantasy or planning of the abuse. The abuse will be described as if it came out of the blue with no warning to the offenders.

> I didn't plan this. I was just watching T.V. by myself, and my niece came into the room and crawled up in my lap. You know

how kids are, she started wriggling around, I told her to stop, but she wouldn't stop. The wriggling caused me to have an erection. After that, I touched her. Nothing like this has ever happened before.

Of course, truly impulsive offenders who have no forewarning that they are going to abuse other people are rare and are not safe to be supervised in the community.

7. **Minimization**—This is similar to the frequency and intrusiveness forms of denial. The offenders in this case will sometimes talk about their abusive behavior as if it were in the past. For example, the incest offender who claims the abuse of his daughter was his way of teaching her about sex and now, after his arrest and conviction, he realizes this was inappropriate and will stop the behavior. This offender will claim that ceasing the behavior will be no problem because he was not being sexual with his daughter through any of his own desires.

Interview Format for Offense History

Interviewing the offender about offense history and sexual history occurs after the personal history has been obtained. Remember the offender has been found guilty by the jury or a judge or has entered a plea of guilty or *nolo contendere*. The purpose of this portion of the interview is to determine the extent of the problem, not to retry the case. In the event there is no disclosure, the offender is not appropriate for community treatment. In these circumstances, it will be necessary to consider community safety and recommend a sentence of incapacitation. Clearly state this to the offender, and do not be surprised if the offender chooses to be more forthright when he realizes that it is not to his advantage to be silent about his offense.

In the event the offender has entered a plea of *nolo contendere*, remember the *nolo contendere* plea does not prevent the offender from discussing the offense with you. In a *nolo* plea, the offender does not deny the facts of the case; he can therefore be held accountable for treatment while being protected in civil court proceedings.

The Alford plea (*North Carolina v. Alford*, 400 U.S. 25, 1970), however, is problematic. The court may accept an Alford plea even while the offender is maintaining his innocence, as long as a factual basis for the offense has been established. Under these circumstances, specialized sex-offender treatment becomes difficult, if not impossible, as the offender is stating he committed no crime and therefore does not have a sexual deviance problem. With the offender in denial, he is not appropriate or amenable for treatment. Educating the district attorney's office to avoid this type of plea with sex offenders is vital, particularly if the district attorney's intent is to recommend probation and specialized sex-offender treatment.

An effective beginning to the interview is a technique developed by Samenow and Yochelson (1977). This strategy involves presenting offenders with a mirror image of themselves. This can be particularly powerful with sex offenders who have built a protective facade, often feeling secure that no one knows who they are or what their secret life entails. When a probation officer begins to explore thoughts and behaviors in the offenders' life that they thought no one knew, it can be disturbing for the offenders; yet, it can provide the opening for more honest disclosure.

To use this technique, the probation officer educates the offender about sex offenders, in general, and dispels common myths. It is important to do this before asking the offenders to discuss their own sexual offense, as it may negate some of the offenders' denial or minimization from the start.

When first using this technique, it may seem a strange and unnecessary step to educate sex offenders about themselves. However, sex offenders often ascribe to the same sex offender stereotypes as other members of the community. As you talk about the characteristics of sex offenders, the prevalent myths concerning them, and the strategies they use to deny the offense, you will be showing your experience and knowledge. Being familiar with the offender's history from your review of the documents will allow you to use examples that are salient for that particular offender. For example, if you were interviewing an incest offender who was in denial, you might begin:

> We have spent the last half hour talking about your personal history, and it is time now to move on to the sexual abuse of your daughter. Over the last year, since your arrest, you have probably wondered numerous times why you abused her.

In this opening statement you are talking as if the abuse is a given. You are attempting to short circuit the delay and digression that occurs with denial.

Do not allow the offender to interrupt you with protestations of innocence. You should continue on and talk about what you know about individuals who sexually abuse their children. It may be helpful to use an example of a denial the offender may have used. For instance, if in the police report the offender is admitting sexual activity with his daughter but states he was only educating her about sex, you could say:

> Some men will rationalize the sexual abuse of their daughter by saying they were only teaching her about sex, that it had absolutely nothing to do with having sexual feelings toward her. We know however, that aside from being wrong and illegal, teaching a child about sex by being sexual with her is not the reason a father initiates or coerces his

daughter to have sex with him. This is a distortion a father may use to justify his actions for a behavior he wants to engage in. It will be important for you to look honestly at yourself. However, it is even more important to learn how to control your urges toward your daughter so the abuse does not continue.

Perhaps, in a different scenario, you are interviewing a young man who raped a woman he met at a party. He has no previous arrests and is not denying he was sexual with her; however, he is denying that it was a rape, and he proceeds to make very degrading statements about the victim to the police:

> People have all kinds of ideas about what a rapist is like. Most people see rapists as sick men who attack women on lonely, deserted streets. They think that if they were to see the rapist in public his looks would reveal his identity as a rapist. In fact, many men know the women they chose to rape. Some men will begin a conversation with a woman at a party for the purpose of manipulating her into being sexual with them later that evening. These men often ignore statements from these women when they indicate they do not want to be sexual.
>
> Some people even think men rape because they are sexually deprived when, in fact, the majority of rapists are engaging in other consenting sexual relationships at the time they commit rape. Probably you think you don't fit the stereotypical image of a rapist. You have a steady job, you have a wife and children, you visit your parents on a weekly basis. So, you may drink a little too much on occasion; it's never been what you would consider out of your control.

Make the examples as relevant to the offender's circumstances as possible. You should emphasize the need for honesty, but at the same time, let the offender know that many offenders initially do deny aspects of their deviant behavior.

It is helpful, strategically, to show empathy by acknowledging the difficulty of the offenders being honest about their hidden sexual abuses. It requires, though, a delicate balance to show the offenders that you have some understanding of their perceived plight without endorsing or colluding with their distortions. These techniques may be more effective with prosocial sex offenders than with sex offenders who have a record of nonsexual criminal offenses in which lying is pervasive throughout all areas of their life.

Many sex offenders do feel out of control with their behavior. Some sex offenders have promised themselves they were not going to sexually abuse again, only to engage in abusive behaviors a few days or a few months later. Before having sex offenders begin to talk about their offense, explain that specialized treatment is available to help them gain control over their abusive behaviors. If sex offenders are going to take the risk of being honest about their behavior, it is important to let them know there is help available.

Interview Strategies to Circumvent Denial

Some of the strategies listed below were drawn from the works of Pithers *et al.* (1989) and McGrath (1990).

Vocabulary—In general, use unambiguous, readily understood vocabulary. Check with offenders to ensure they understand you. This is particularly important with lower-functioning offenders who may have a limited vocabulary. Some offenders use only slang to describe sexual activity; as long as the slang is not derogatory, it is acceptable to use their terms during a presentence investigation. Time is limited, and it could be confusing for the offender to cope with unfamiliar words, terms, or expressions. For example, one offender did not know the meaning of mastur-bation and used the slang expression of "jerking off" to describe masturbation.

Ask direct questions—It is important to ask questions in a straightforward man-ner. In turn, the offenders may be more direct in their responses. This method provides a way of modeling behavior you are expecting from the offender. For example, during a presentence interview, one offender was asked, routinely, if he ever had been sexually victimized. The offender leaned back in his chair, paused, and said, "I've been waiting for someone to ask me that." This man had both a psychiatric and a psychological evaluation, and the question of prior victimiza-tion had not been asked. The offender went on to report victimization as a young teenager, over a four-year period. The offender expressed little anxiety discussing the abuse, but it was clear that this was information that unless asked would not be volunteered.

Use behavioral descriptors—Avoid words such as "molest," "rapist," or "pedophile," and do not allow offenders to use these words when giving a state-ment. Behaviors should be described. For example, one offender was adamant that he had not "molested" his niece. It was only later that the probation officer discovered the offender thought "molest" meant he had penetrated his niece's vagina with his penis. The victim's statement in this case described her uncle touching her breast and vaginal area but no penetration.

Emphasize what happened not why it happened—Sex offenders often think that if they can understand why they sexually abused, that will enable them to control their behavior. For the purposes of the presentence investigation, it is more helpful for case planning to know what offenders did, rather than to listen to the explanations of why offenders think they did it.

Attempt to develop a "Yes" response set—Ask offenders questions early on that result in agreement so that, later in the interview, when more difficult questions are asked, there may be less resistance from them. For example, discuss offenders' personal and social history before asking them about sexual offenses (which are more threatening and likely will bring some resistance).

Do not make denial easy for the offender—Avoid questions that illicit yes or no responses, particularly questions that offenders may deny, thinking it will make them look better. Therefore, avoid phrasing questions such as, "Do you . . .?" or "Have you ever . . .?" as these words provide an easy avenue for the offender to deny the question. Instead, ask, "How long have you . . .?" or "How often do you . . .?" or "When did you first . . .?" Phrasing the question this way, you are implying that a certain activity took place, and what you want to know is how long, how often, and so on. If, indeed, it is activity the offenders have never indulged in, they can clearly state that, but their answer will need to be more than the one-word reply of "no."

Repeat questions—Repeating the same question during the interview often will elicit further disclosure. For this reason, ask offenders to go through their offense statement at least twice. Asking the same question in different ways also may elicit more disclosure.

Do not reduce anxiety—The uncertainty of court disposition during the presentence investigation can be very stressful for the offender. This stress may lead to more honest disclosure.

Use of religion to avoid responsibility—Some sex offenders use their religious affiliation to support their denial. Other offenders use their new-found (and sometimes insincere) religious beliefs to minimize the difficulty of change. Because of the number of sex offenders who misuse and manipulate their faith, there may be a tendency to discount any offender who expresses religious beliefs. This should be avoided. For those offenders who are sincere, their faith may be beneficial in the change process. With information regarding sexual abuse, a religious/spiritual leader can be extremely beneficial in supporting offenders as they take full responsibility and engage meaningfully in treatment.

Do not tip your hand—It is important to convey to offenders the thoroughness with which you have reviewed all the available information. However, do not be specific. Most offenders will have reviewed with their defense attorney the facts that are known to the district attorney. With this knowledge, they may try to simulate an openness that is not genuine. Or, they may subtly test the interviewer as to how vague they can be without being called on it. Such tactics will enable the probation officer to evaluate offenders' level of honesty. For example, is the offender only giving you information you already know from your review of the documents, or is the offender adding information you did not know previously?

Accept rationalization and minimization if it serves your purpose—It is not necessary to challenge offenders each time they rationalize or minimize their behavior if they are beginning to disclose. In fact, if each distortion is confronted, offenders may close down. Such actions may interrupt the flow of the interview and prevent you from acquiring additional information. This is one of the important distinctions between the assessment for the presentence report and the supervision of the sex offender. There will be sufficient time to confront distortions during the course of supervision.

Confront contradictions—If offenders are providing inconsistent information, the probation officer should seek clarity. This confrontation can be indirect ("There's just one thing I don't understand. Do you remember when you said . . .") or more direct ("Your statement confuses me. First you said . . . then you said . . .").

Mix supportive comments with confrontation—It is appropriate and recommended that offenders receive supportive comments from the probation officer when they are being honest and are taking responsibility for their actions. At the same time, they need to be held accountable when they are not.

Ask "successive-approximation" questions—There may be a wide difference between the offenders' statements of what occurred and the police report. Using this technique, you will be asking the offenders questions that will draw them closer to what is stated in the police report. For example, the victim has reported vaginal penetration, but the offender admits only fondling, over her nightgown. The questioning may be directed in the following way: "You know how kids toss and turn at night. How many times did you find your daughter's nightgown up around her hips . . . and when that occurred, how often did you stroke her bare thigh . . .?" As you get admission on these points, you may continue the questioning until you encounter some resistance. It is important to move slowly. When you come across resistance, it is okay to move to another line of questioning and return to this topic at a later time.

Offense History Questions

How offenders talk about their offense can indicate the degree of responsibility they are taking for the offense. How sex offenders choose to offend gives information as to their threat to the community and their suitability for community supervision. Knowing the offense characteristics helps in determining what special conditions of probation will be necessary for community supervision. You want not only the factual details of the offense itself, but the planning, the selecting of victim, and the grooming or stalking that preceded the offense.

At the beginning of the presentence report, there is a summary of the offense that primarily will be from the police report. This summary should describe in detail the assaultive behaviors, the location and duration of the assault, and how the offender gained access to the victim. The age and sex of the offender and the victim is included in this section as is the relationship between the two. Trauma to the victim should be included as well as when and how the victim disclosed the offense.

The offense statements taken from offenders should be detailed and in the offenders' own words. This statement should begin at the planning stage, proceed through the offense itself, and end with the offenders' attitude and feelings about what they did.

With a rapist who had no prior relationship with the victim, have the offender describe the entire day leading up to the assault. This begins to establish the risk factors that precede the assault. With an incest offender, it will be important to establish the sometimes lengthy grooming that preceded the hands-on abuse. Depending on the duration of the abuse, the time frame may begin months or years before the actual offense of record.

Obviously, the depth of offenders' statements will depend on how open they are. However, if offenders are denying or minimizing the abuse, the statement should reflect this. Summarize the contradictions between the police report and the offenders' statements, should this be the case.

In the shaded box are questions that can be asked of offenders as they are giving their statement. These questions can be elaborated on and do not have to be asked in sequence. It is important to note that some questions will not be relevant for certain types of offenders.

1. Where did the assault take place? How did the offender get there? Was the location randomly selected? Is the location always the same, such as the victim's bedroom? Describe in detail.

2. How did the offender select the victim? Was it opportunistic (the victim was in the wrong place at the wrong time)? Was it planned (the victim was known to the offender)? What characteristics did the victim have that resulted in the offender's selection (sex, age, physical or emotional attributes)?

3. How did the offender force the victim to submit? For example, did the offender use verbal threats, enticements, intimidation, trickery, physical abuse, a weapon or a threat to harm persons close to the victim?

4. What was the victim's reaction? Did the victim say anything? Was the victim scared, crying, passive, submissive, or combative? How emotionally removed is the offender from the pain of the victim? Did the offender stop at anytime because of the victim's reaction?

5. What was arousing to the offender? For example, did the victim's resistance to the rape arouse the offender? Was the physical assault arousing? Was the submissiveness of the victim arousing? Were the physical characteristics of the victim arousing?

6. What did the offender say to the victim? Did the offender, for example, use threatening, foul, humiliating, or instructional language? Did the offender use secrecy, threats, or bribes to keep the victim from disclosing?

7. Were alcohol or drugs used? If so, for what purpose: to entice the victim, to reduce victim resistance, or to reduce the offender's own inhibitions? Were other enticements used such as money?

8. What did the offender want to do but did not? Why not?

9. Was a weapon visible but not used? Why? If the weapon was used, how was it used?

10. How did the offender feel after the assault was over?

11. Has the offender ever attempted to stop the abusive behavior? How?

Having the offender go through the offense at least twice may lead to more detail from the offender and will allow for questioning of the gaps in the first statement. It is not uncommon for a sex offender who is beginning to disclose to leave out the more violent or intrusive aspects of the offense. Being familiar with the police report enables the interviewer to be aware of these gaps and ask pointed questions.

For example, if a rapist admits the assault but leaves out the weapon he used, a probation officer could say: "I would like you to go through the details of the offense again, and this time I want to know when you took out the knife and how you used it during the assault." This statement allows the offender to know the probation officer is aware of the knife, without calling him an outright liar. This phrasing is used to avoid putting offenders on the defensive and reducing disclosure.

Sexual History Questions

This section of the presentence report is usually the most awkward for probation officers because they do not ask such personal questions of an offender who has not committed a sexual offense. However, with sex offenders, it is essential to ask questions that pertain to their deviant and nondeviant sexual history.

Imagine trying to determine the extent of offenders' drinking problems and not asking them detailed questions about their use of alcohol. With a problem drinker, you ask when the drinking began, the amount of consumption, the circumstances leading to the abusive drinking, and the history of the family's alcohol use. With sex offenders, close questioning about their sexual history is essential.

Questions such as how they learned about sex, and what their parents told them about sex, will provide information about their upbringing that may not have come out during the earlier interviewing on family history. Asking offenders when they first realized they were different sexually approaches the early, developing pattern of sexually abusive behavior. Remember to ask open-ended questions so as to avoid clipped yes or no responses. For example, ask offenders *when* they started to masturbate, not *if* they masturbate.

Questions Related to Sexual History

1. How did you learn about sex?
2. What did your parents tell you about sex?
3. When did you start to date? Tell me about your first sexual experience.
4. How old were you when you started to masturbate? What are your fantasies? Have they changed over time?
5. How often do you masturbate? What did your parents tell you about masturbation?
6. How old were you when you realized that things were not quite right for you sexually? How old were you when the sexual problems began?
7. Describe your sexual relationship with your spouse/significant other. How often do you engage in sexual activity? Who initiates sex?
8. Have you ever been a victim of sexual abuse? What is the first sexual experience you remember as a child? Have you ever been scared or humiliated sexually. How? When?

Offenders should be questioned in detail about all prior arrests or convictions. The record check and any further information obtained on these convictions will aid in this questioning.

Question offenders about whether they have been sexually victimized. It is not unusual for offenders to deny having been sexually abused as a child, but when asked to describe their first sexual experience, they describe a sexual victimization. The seriousness of the abusive behavior of sex offenders is not mitigated by their having been sexually abused. Although being victimized rarely has an impact on determining level of supervision, this is important information to pass on to the therapist.

Closing the Interview

Explain again to offenders at this point that the presentence report will follow them for many years to come; therefore, establishing their credibility as honest people is important. Let them know, if after the interview is over, they want to correct any misinformation they should call you. This shows the offenders that you are aware of the battle that may be going on in inside of them around the issue of how honest to be.

If offenders take responsibility, the probation officer should acknowledge the important first step they have taken in stopping their abusive behavior. Remind offenders of the importance of honesty for effective treatment, and that treatment is available to help them gain control over their deviant behavior. By letting offenders know they will have other opportunities to discuss their sexual history, you are indicating to offenders your expectation of more disclosures.

If offenders have made new disclosures during the interview, seal the interview. Sealing an interview means making offenders aware that they may feel anxiety because of how much of their secret life they have just disclosed. Preparing offenders for this anxiety may prevent a future recantation. Let the offenders know this is a normal reaction and tell them to remember that the anxiety will decrease over time. Letting the offenders know in advance what they may experience after leaving your office may insure that their disclosure remains intact (William Pithers, personal communication 1987).

Summary and Recommendation of Presentence Investigation Report

The function of the summary and recommendation portion of a presentence investigation report is to assess the level of risk offenders present to the community as well as their amenability to specialized treatment and the special conditions of probation needed for supervision, if community placement is recommended.

First, all pertinent information should be highlighted and summarized. Avoid simply repeating prior statements. Point out the contradictions, if any, between offenders' statements and the police reports and the victims' statements. Emphasize aggravating and mitigating factors of the offense.

Next, summarize the offenders' strengths and weaknesses as they relate to their risk for reoffense. Assess their motivation to reduce their potential for reoffending. Remember, it is important to be as clear about the offenders' strengths as it is their weaknesses. Finally, the summary should address amenability to treatment, risk to the community, special conditions of probation related to reducing risk, and restitution to the victim.

Amenability to Treatment

Ideally, the sex offender will be undergoing a psychosexual evaluation at the same time the presentence investigation is occurring, allowing for early collaboration between therapist and probation officer in case planning. It also allows the probation officer to compare notes around inconsistencies or contradictions by the offender. Although there will be overlap in the reports, the emphasis for the therapist will be on evaluating amenability to treatment and creating a treatment plan. The emphasis for the probation officer will be on evaluating level of risk, appropriateness for community supervision, and the special court-imposed conditions of probation needed to control risk.

The reality, however, is that psychosexual evaluations often are not ordered in conjunction with the presentence investigation report, and the probation officer must make a preliminary determination of amenability to treatment. If the probation officer is not collaborating with a therapist during the presentence investigation, the probation officer should answer the following questions in determining amenability to treatment:

Amenability to Treatment

1. Does the offender admit to the offense and accept responsibility for his or her actions?
2. Does the offender acknowledge to some extent that his or her behavior has had harmful consequences for the victim?
3. Does the offender identify the behavior as a problem and express a desire to change?
4. Does the offender agree to participate in specialized treatment to address his or her deviant behavior?
5. Does the offender agree to abide by the special conditions of probation that are recommended by the probation officer?

Sex offenders rarely take total responsibility for their actions at the time of the presentence report. Therefore, the probation officer will be evaluating where offenders are in the process of accepting responsibility, and their openness to the specialized treatment that will assist them in changing their deviant behaviors. Specialized sex-offender treatment should be explained fully to offenders and to their attorneys, especially if their attorneys are inexperienced in this area. If there is treatment in your district, include a copy of the treatment contract (see page 132) with the presentence report. This can prevent later concerns by defendants or their attorneys that they had no idea the treatment was so intrusive and, if they had, they never would have agreed to it.

The availability of specialized treatment for sex offenders is critical. If appropriate treatment is not available, it will be difficult for offenders to learn and use strategies for behavioral self-control. If the sex offender is placed on probation without specialized treatment, the probation officer is in the position of controlling risk through supervision. Reducing risk will occur by the offender engaging in treatment. There will be situations, though, in which offenders may be amenable to treatment but pose a risk to the community to such a degree that treatment must take place in prison or in a residential setting.

Level of Risk to the Community

The standard risk assessment instruments used by correctional departments are not effective in assessing the risk a sex offender poses to the community because many sex offenders do not have the criminal histories or chaotic lifestyles that the standard risk instruments use to determine risk. Currently, there is not a validated risk assessment instrument for sex offenders. In the Addendum (page 145) is a copy of the Vermont Assessment of Sex Offender Risk developed by McGrath and Hoke (1994). This instrument is in the process of being validated.

In determining the risk the sex offender presents, it is necessary to address the types of offenses committed, sexual history, treatment history, and amenability to treatment. The probation officer also must evaluate the available supervision resources which will allow for appropriate field supervision and networking within the community. This includes electronic surveillance, plethysmograph, polygraph, specialized treatment, and caseload size.

Sentencing options vary across jurisdictions. Some states have mandatory sentences for particular offenses while other states allow for wider flexibility. Some states use incarceration more frequently than other states, not only for risk control, but for retribution and deterrence. For purposes of this section, incarceration versus probation will be addressed by looking at the aggravating and mitigating variables pertaining to risk to the community. It will not address incarceration for purposes of retribution and deterrence, or the different sentencing guidelines that vary from jurisdiction to jurisdiction.

Aggravating and Mitigating Variables

The variety of issues that go into determining the risk a particular sex offender poses can make the recommendation process difficult. The incest offender who has taken responsibility, moved out of his home so his victim can remain with the family, expressed concern about the harm his behaviors have caused, and has started specialized treatment, is easy to assess as amenable to treatment and appropriate for community supervision. The offender who rapes a woman at knifepoint is easy to assess as well: he goes to prison. The violent nature of the act coupled with the use of a weapon makes this situation clear.

Most assessment procedures are not, lamentably, so clear-cut. What about the twice-convicted child molester who is taking responsibility for the offense but who has never been in specialized treatment before? What about the offender who has a stable job, the support of his family, no prior record, but who is in total denial of his two convictions for exhibitionism?

Obviously, with all the variables, there is no set formula for determining the appropriate disposition to ensure offenders' rehabilitation and the safety of the community. Each assessment is unique and must be approached as such. It also is important to identify offenders who are not amenable for treatment so a sentence of incarceration for purposes of incapacitation can be recommended, for community safety is vital.

McGrath (1992) suggests there are two general strategies for assessing risk. The primary strategy addresses the offender's similarity to other types of offenders, the assumption being that predicting future behavior is easier if we know how other offenders with similar characteristics behave. The secondary strategy addresses the more individualized assessment of the offender. Consider the following information on an offender:

> A young man in his thirties has been convicted of fondling preteen boys; he has, approximately, a ten-year history of this behavior with little escalation into more intrusive behaviors, such as oral-genital contact or penetration. He has never been involved in a consenting sexual relationship with an adult. When interviewed, the offender takes responsibility for his actions, and states he has, on two occasions, gone to the crisis clinic for help. He was not entirely honest at the clinic, due to embarrassment and fear of arrest, and did not return for treatment. His mother and sister believe he is guilty and remain supportive of him. As with many sex offenders, this man has no prior record, no alcohol or drug problem and has been employed at the same job for fifteen years. The type of offense—male offender abusing a male child—indicates he has twice the risk of reoffending than if the victim were female (McGrath 1991, Quinsey *et al.* 1993). The individualized assessment of the offender shows the following positive factors: taking responsibility for his actions; a supportive, noncolluding family; and attempting to seek help at the crisis clinic (verified by the probation officer).

obation officer preparing the presentence investigation report on this und him amenable to treatment. He also determined him to be appropriate for community supervision under the following conditions: specialized sex-offender treatment, no association with children under the age of eighteen, disclosure of offense to his employer, and disclosure of offense to the neighbors. The mother and sister, in addition, agreed to be part of the supervision network (see page 39). The court placed this offender on probation with the above special conditions. He remained in treatment for four years and received a satisfactory termination. Six years after finishing treatment, there have been no subsequent arrests or investigations of this offender.

McGrath (1992) recommends focusing the assessment of risk on five factors.

(1) probability of reoffense
(2) degree of harm most likely to result from a reoffense
(3) conditions under which reoffense is most likely to occur
(4) likely victims of a reoffense
(5) time frame in which a reoffense is most likely to occur

These five factors provide a helpful organizational format for a probation officer to follow in assessing risk, managing risk, and determining the special conditions of probation (if probation is recommended).

1. What is the probability of reoffense?

Determining probability of reoffense requires examining the offender's similarity to other types of sex offenders. Offense type, multiple paraphilias, degree of force, criminal lifestyle, and deviant sexual arousal are characteristics to be considered in the probability of reoffense. Examining the highlights of McGrath's (1991) review of sex offender risk studies is helpful at this juncture.

Offense type: The review of offense type risk studies is helpful in determining the probable degree of risk each sex offender type poses in relationship to each other. However, in his review, McGrath found only two studies that compared more than three offense types in a single study. With that said, McGrath found that untreated exhibitionists had the highest recidivism rates and rapists the second highest. Both McGrath (1991) and Quinsey *et al.* (1995) in their recidivism reviews on child molesters found that child molesters who abused unrelated boys had higher recidivism rates than those who abused unrelated girls. The incest offender had the lowest recidivism rates among all the types of child offenders.

Multiple paraphilias: Offenders with multiple paraphilias or sexual disorders have higher rates of recidivism than offenders with a single paraphilia. For example, in one study, Abel and his colleagues (Abel *et al.* 1987) enrolled 192 child molesters into a structured treatment program. Ninety-eight subjects were followed for one year after treatment, and the overall recidivism rate was 12.2 percent. However, for those offenders who abused both males and females and both children and adolescents, the recidivism rate was 75 percent.

In addition, offenders whose pretreatment sexual offense history included hands-off offenses, such as exhibitionism and peeping, reoffended at a higher rate than offenders without such a history. The preliminary results of a recidivism study in Vermont show similar results. Non-incest offenders abusing both female and male children reoffended at a rate of 55 percent compared to 10–11 percent for offenders who abused only female or only male children.

Degree of force: Use of force by sex offenders is an indicator of increased risk to reoffend (Marshall and Barbaree 1988). Of particularly high risk are those offenders who are aroused sexually by aggression and sadism (Groth and Birnbaum 1979). Unless the offender is unusually self-disclosing during the interview, the fusion of sexual arousal and aggression will be difficult to detect without a penile plethysmograph assessment, which measures erectile responses in males and records their arousal patterns.

Sexual arousal: McGrath (1991) reviewed seven studies that looked at deviant sexual arousal and recidivism. Six of the seven studies reviewed showed a positive correlation between deviant sexual arousal and recidivism. Quinsey *et al.* (1995) found similar results and concluded that there is evidence that deviant arousal is related to recidivism. McGrath (1991) cautions that "although phallometric measures should never stand alone as predictors of sexual recidivism, in combination with other variables, they provide an important data source."

Criminal lifestyle: Offenders who have a prior criminal record always have been at higher risk to reoffend than offenders with no prior criminal record. Sex offenders are no different in this regard: sex offenders who have prior sexual convictions also pose a higher risk of reoffending (Quinsey *et al.* 1995).

2. What degree of harm would most likely result from a reoffense?

If offenders have a history of acting violently, they have a higher risk for future violent behavior. Obviously, the use of a weapon raises the risk of harm to a very high degree. Asking about the offender's masturbatory fantasies and whether there is a preference for violence or sadism is important, although many offenders may not be honest under this line of questioning. Nonetheless, ask. Warren *et al.* (1991) found "that the presence of excessive bindings, transportation of the victim to a different location, and sustained contact may be associated with an exacerbation in violence among a select sample of serial rapists." This finding points to the importance of reviewing all police reports in detail.

However, if there is no history of violent behavior, examine carefully the offender's pattern of past offenses for any increase in intrusiveness or threats of violence. For example, is the voyeur now entering homes that are occupied, or is the child molester making threats to physically harm the victim for not cooperating when previously financial bribes were used?

3. What are the conditions under which a reoffense is most likely to occur?

This is a critical question for the probation officer in deciding not only the special conditions of probation, but whether an incarcerative sentence will be necessary to control risk. The issue is not only offenders' amenability to treatment, but their self-control and willingness to abide by the special conditions of probation.

The other issue to consider is the ability of the probation officer to provide the level of supervision that will detect noncompliance. The purpose of treatment is to have offenders reach the point of managing their own deviant sexual impulses. This can take months, even with the most willing offenders. Meanwhile, if offenders are to remain in the community, they must be willing to abide by the specialized conditions set forth in the probation warrant aimed at controlling their risk. The probation officer must be able to provide the close supervision that will detect noncompliance.

During the presentence investigation, the probation officer needs to identify the risk factors that precede the offense. The next step is to identify what conditions of probation are necessary for monitoring and controlling these risk factors. Even after a psychosexual evaluation and a presentence report, there is much to learn about offenders as they engage in the treatment process. It is best to be cautious by providing a high level of structure. Loosening the structure of probation over time is easier than tightening the structure after a problem surfaces.

Risk factors to consider

> **Victim Access:** It is generally accepted practice that child molesters, including incest offenders, should be denied any contact with minor children at the beginning of probation supervision. As treatment progresses, the therapist and the probation officer will determine together how, when, and if this restriction is to be lessened. The ability of the probation officer to effectively monitor this restriction will be essential.

> **Substance Abuse:** Alcohol and/or drugs do not cause a sex offender to abuse, but they can act as disinhibitors. It is recommended that sex offenders initially

not be allowed to use or possess alcohol at all regardless of whether it has been a problem for them, for the following reasons:

—Treatment is stressful and the offender who has no history of abusive drinking may resort to misusing alcohol to relieve the stress of changing ingrained patterns.

—The offender may be successful in hiding an alcohol problem that is not identified at the time of the presentence report.

—Restricting possession will address the child molesters who do not have a problem with alcohol but use alcohol to access children.

With this condition, the roommate-partner-spouse of the sex offender will no longer be able to drink at home or keep alcoholic beverages in the home. Interview the other adults in the residence to determine if they will comply with the alcohol restriction imposed on the offender.

The seriousness of the offender's alcohol/drug problem will determine if the offender is referred elsewhere for an alcohol/drug assessment and/or treatment. It is important to assess the offender's ability to abstain from alcohol/drugs, as sex-offender treatment will be seriously compromised if the offender is abusing alcohol and/or drugs.

Sexually Stimulating Material: Determining what is sexually arousing will vary from offender to offender. The probation officer must consider information learned during the presentence process, along with details of the offense, to determine what materials must not be possessed by the offender. For example, a catalogue showing pictures of preadolescent children in underwear is arousing to some pedophiles. Some offenders use erotica for masturbatory fantasies while other offenders will use it to access potential victims. For example, an offender may leave *Penthouse* magazine around his home and gauge the reaction of his potential victim when he or she comes across it, or he may show pornographic videos as a prelude to the abuse.

Employment and Residence: Assess whether the offender's current employment or residence places potential victims at risk. For the child molester, jobs at elementary schools or residences that are next door to a daycare center would be forbidden. Similarly, a residence in which the housemate has an extended family with children who are continually dropping by on weekends would be deemed inappropriate.

Assessing risk at jobs and residences requires a field visit and contact with employers, landlords, and housemates. It may be necessary for the offender to change jobs or residence for probation to be a sentencing option. Offenders who are self-employed will need careful scrutiny, especially if their employment allows for long hours in which there is no accountability for offenders' use of their time and whereabouts, such as driving a truck. The probation officer needs the authority through conditions of probation to authorize all residences and employment (see Probation and Parole Conditions, page 127).

Use of Vehicle: Assess whether offenders used their automobile to cruise for potential victims. This may be more prevalent with exhibitionists and rapists than with child molesters. However, offenders who abuse teenage boys may also choose to own cars that are especially appealing to teenage boys. For example, an offender may use his red convertible Mustang to entice a teenage boy into conversation as a grooming technique for future abuse.

Emotional State: Pithers *et al.* (1989) analyzed case records of 200 clients and found that anger was a common emotional precursor for rapists, while depression was the more common emotional precursor for child molesters. Losing a job and/or relationship can be a particularly high-risk time for the sex offender. Monitoring emotional states will necessitate close coordination with the treatment provider and supervision network.

The importance of specialized sex-offender treatment cannot be emphasized enough. Marshall and Barbaree (1988) found that for those offenders who remain untreated, there is no difference in reoffense rates between sex offenders who admit and those who deny their offenses. The supervision of the sex offender must remain intensive, at least at the beginning, even for those offenders who accept responsibility for their actions, are found amenable for treatment, and appear compliant.

When evaluating the conditions under which a reoffense may occur, it may be determined that the conditions are too numerous and/or difficult to monitor safely. In these cases, despite the offenders' amenability to treatment, the risk they pose is too great, and an incarcerated sentence will be necessary.

4. Who would be the likely victims of a reoffense?

It is important to review an offender's police record to assess potential victims. Determining likely victims of a reoffense, however, involves more than looking at an offender's instant offense or his or her conviction record. Some sex offenders do engage in multiple deviant behaviors. Some incest offenders have a history of offending children outside the home and even of rape (Becker and Coleman 1988, see especially page 87 for a summary of this research).

Plethysmographs and polygraphs can be helpful in determining if other types of victims may be at risk. Although there are some sex offenders who engage in only one type of deviant behavior, a significant percentage engage in multiple deviant behaviors. In the interviewing and the supervising of the offender, it is always best to assume there is more, not less, in offenders' sexual history.

5. When is a reoffense most likely to occur?

A probation officer, when deciding on special conditions and method of supervision, needs to address the variables involved in the probable timing of a reoffense. Frisbie (1969) followed a group of sex offenders released from Atascadero State Hospital over a five-year period. She found that rapists were at the highest risk to reoffend during the first nine months after being released from prison, with the rate of reoffense decreasing each year after.

However, child molesters, including incest offenders, were found to be at their highest risk to reoffend two to three years after their release from prison, perhaps because of the lengthy grooming techniques used by many child molesters.

A more recent study by Quinsey *et al.* (1995) reviewed a group of rapists and child molesters released from a maximum-security psychiatric facility and found that the risk was as great in the seventh year as it was in the first year. They did find that rapists were a greater risk than child molesters during the follow-up period. This has important ramifications for supervision. It shows the importance and necessity of lengthy probation or parole supervision for rapists, child molesters, and incest offenders.

Taking into account such considerations as time of day, season of the year, and offender age also can help the probation officer in developing strategies of supervision designed to prevent reoffenses. According to the U.S. Department of Justice (1985) two-thirds of all rapes and attempted rapes occur at night, while exhibitionists tend to commit their offenses during daylight hours. Curfews for rapists will be important in reducing the risk of reoffense while for exhibitionists, curfews may have little impact.

Conclusion

The presentence investigation report provides the probation officer with the opportunity to educate the legal system, impact sentencing, and plan what specialized probation conditions will be important to maintain community safety. In planning a systems approach to the treatment and supervision of the sex offender, the presentence investigation has a crucial role. For parole officers, and for probation officers who have not had the opportunity to complete a presentence investigation, this chapter can be used during the intake interview and for case planning.

Chapter 2

Relapse Prevention as a Supervision Strategy

Experience shows that standard supervision practices with sex offenders are ineffective. Sex offenders typically present few management problems. They hold jobs, keep their appointments, and complete the conditions of probation, so rarely is a problem obvious until after arrest on a new charge. The standard conditions of probation/parole do not provide the officer sufficient leeway to intervene when there is a problem. This would certainly be the case with the child molester who marries a woman with three children. In this instance, standard conditions of probation/parole generally do not provide the probation/parole officer the authority to curtail the relationship or to protect the children from potential danger. A different model of supervision that accounts for various areas of risk is imperative.

The strategy of supervision proposed is a combination of three techniques: relapse prevention, specialized conditions of probation/parole tailored to the offender's risk areas, and use of a collateral community network.

Relapse prevention is a self-management program designed to teach individuals who are trying to change their behaviors to identify problems early on and to develop strategies to avoid or cope more effectively with these problems to avoid a relapse (Marlatt and Gordon 1980). This model was initially developed as a treatment tool with addictive behaviors such as substance abuse, gambling, and smoking. In the early 1980s, William Pithers, Janice Marques *et al.* (1983) adapted the model for treatment of sex offenders. A further adaptation was made to include a supervisory dimension that includes probation/parole officers and develops a collateral network of community members (Pithers *et al.* 1988).

This chapter addresses educating the offender in the relapse prevention method; developing the collateral network and the supervision case plan; ongoing supervision; supervising offenders in denial; and assisting the offender in the transition from an incarcerated program. Several important principles should guide the probation/parole officer who uses the relapse prevention model with sex offenders.

First, treatment will not cure sex offenders of their sexual deviancy; they can learn skills enabling them to stop their abusive behavior, but treatment will not eradicate the deviant interests. Therefore, offenders always must be prepared for the possibility of a return of deviant interests.

Second, offenders must be active participants in identifying risky behaviors and developing the coping strategies to address them.

Third, the self-report of risky behavior by sex offenders historically has been unreliable; therefore, it is essential to develop an informed collateral network.

Fourth, the responsibility squarely rests with offenders for curtailing their sexually deviant impulses. Treatment is not magical, and if offenders choose to remain in denial or refuse to engage in treatment to reduce their deviant interests, they are at high risk to reengage in sexually deviant behaviors.

Educating Offenders in Relapse Prevention

The first step in teaching the relapse prevention model is to have offenders identify the precursors to their sexually deviant behavior. Precursors are the events that happen prior to committing a sexual offense; it includes seemingly unimportant decisions, maladaptive coping responses, risk factors, lapses, and the abstinence violation effect. These terms will be defined in the following pages.

Begin the process of educating offenders by having them describe what set of circumstances or emotions occurred prior to the commission of the offense. Make it clear that while the behavior is not an excuse for the offense, it may have started a sequence of events leading to the offense. Therefore, having the offender recount the circumstances preceding the offense is the beginning of "owning" the process of offending.

Seemingly Unimportant Decisions

In identifying precursors, the link to seemingly unimportant decisions is made. A seemingly unimportant decision (SUD) is a decision that, at first, appears to have little bearing on a lapse or relapse. These decisions taken by themselves may appear unimportant. However, inserted into a chain of events, they take on important meaning.

> Lee, twenty-eight, had been convicted of molesting a twelve-year-old girl. He had a substance abuse problem, but had been abstinent since being placed on probation. Aside from working, Lee was involved in sex-offender treatment, Alcoholics Anonymous meetings, and had enrolled part-time at the local community college. He was maintaining a relationship with a woman, Nan, who he had met before his arrest. His home life was stressful; the few hours he had to spend with Nan were spent bickering over finances. To reduce stress, Lee began to jog before AA to help block thoughts of drinking, and the problems in his relationship.

Relapse Prevention Model

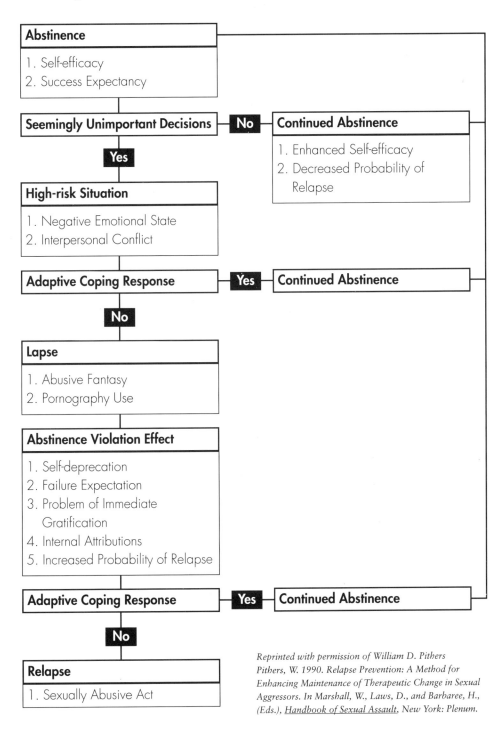

Abstinence
1. Self-efficacy
2. Success Expectancy

Seemingly Unimportant Decisions — **No** → **Continued Abstinence**
1. Enhanced Self-efficacy
2. Decreased Probability of Relapse

Yes

High-risk Situation
1. Negative Emotional State
2. Interpersonal Conflict

Adaptive Coping Response — **Yes** — **Continued Abstinence**

No

Lapse
1. Abusive Fantasy
2. Pornography Use

Abstinence Violation Effect
1. Self-deprecation
2. Failure Expectation
3. Problem of Immediate Gratification
4. Internal Attributions
5. Increased Probability of Relapse

Adaptive Coping Response — **Yes** — **Continued Abstinence**

No

Relapse
1. Sexually Abusive Act

Reprinted with permission of William D. Pithers
Pithers, W. 1990. Relapse Prevention: A Method for
Enhancing Maintenance of Therapeutic Change in Sexual
Aggressors. In Marshall, W., Laws, D., and Barbaree, H.,
(Eds.), Handbook of Sexual Assault, New York: Plenum.

Taken out of context, the jogging appeared harmless, even healthy. However, for Lee it was the beginning of a sequence of events that led to a potential relapse, given the other stressors occurring in his life. Lee was taking on too much responsibility with work and school, yet he was unwilling to make any changes to his routine. At AA meetings and sex-offender treatment, Lee was not talking about the stress he felt or the arguments with his partner, Nan. Earlier patterns of overextending himself, refusing to compromise, and keeping thoughts and feelings to himself began to reemerge.

> Lee had convinced himself that jogging in the evening helped relieve stress and reduced the tensions at home, school, and work. He rationalized that jogging was a healthy alternative. Instead, the jogging resulted in further isolation from the issues that were contributing to the stress in his life, clearly a risk factor for Lee.

Lee had made the first in a series of seemingly unimportant decisions. He made a conscious choice to overlook his increasing workload at school and work, and added to it by beginning evening jogs. For a sex offender with his history, Lee's avoidance of the stresses reemerging in his life placed him in a high-risk situation.

Risk Factors

A risk factor is a set of internal stimuli or external circumstances that threaten offenders' sense of self-control and thus increase the risk of lapse or relapse. Failure to deal successfully with those circumstances will bring offenders one step closer to a potential relapse. This is a critical point in the chain of events. Offenders can choose a number of adaptive coping responses to remove themselves from the high-risk situation or they can continue in their relapse process, heightening the risk of reoffense (maladaptive coping response).

> One particular morning, Lee had another disagreement with Nan resulting in her walking out on Lee. All day Lee was depressed. Several times he attempted to call Nan but was unable to reach her. Upon returning home, Lee found Nan had not yet returned. Anxious, he called a few places where she might be, but none of her friends had seen her that evening. Lee decided to go for a run to think about what he was going to do.
> On a number of occasions while jogging in the evenings, Lee passed a park and would see a young girl who frequently sat alone on one of the benches. Lee began to think about her, imagining that she might speak to him if he ran by her. With that thought in mind, Lee cut his

route short, heading to the park where he had seen the girl. Approaching the park, he could see she was not on the bench, so he decided to run further and come by the park later. Lee ran down a number of side streets, circled the block and on the next pass by the park, he saw the girl approaching the bench. He stopped running to position himself by a set of large evergreens while he watched her.

Lee was, at this point, in the middle of his relapse process. His seemingly unimportant decision was to go for an evening run while he was depressed, and in fact, he headed directly for the park where he had previously seen a young girl. He had placed himself squarely in the middle of a high-risk situation.

Maladaptive Coping Response

Lee had employed a maladaptive coping response in the manner he chose to address his depression. A maladaptive coping response is an effort to deal with a risk factor or lapse which actually brings the offender closer to relapse.

Adaptive Coping Response

Lee could have chosen an adaptive coping response defined as an effort to deal with a risk factor or lapse that acts to help the offender avoid a relapse. In this case, he could have called his AA sponsor or a support person rather than placing himself in a situation with a potential victim. In failing to deal appropriately with his depression, Lee moved a step closer to a possible relapse and, in fact, entered into a further step along the relapse continuum.

Lapse

A lapse is an emotion, fantasy, thought, or behavior that is part of the offender's cycle and relapse pattern. Lapses are not sex offenses. They are precursors or risk factors for sex offenses. In thinking about the young girl in the park, Lee began to fantasize about her and the possibility of her speaking with him. As he began to think about how he might engage her in conversation, Lee was actively in a lapse. It should be highlighted that lapses are to be expected and should be anticipated by the offender and the probation/parole officer.

However, an offender must employ particular problem-solving and self-control skills to successfully manage a lapse. Lee was at a crossroads. He could exit the situation he had placed himself in and return home, or he could remain where he was and continue in the steps that could potentially lead to relapse.

Lee began thinking about how depressed he was and what he might do to make Nan come home. He began to imagine a number of scenarios involving the young girl on the bench and wondered what she was thinking at this moment. Lee looked over at the girl on the bench and could feel his heart pounding. He began to think about merely talking with the girl because she looked so sad.

Abstinence Violation Effect

In engaging in his lapse, Lee encountered a series of changes in his beliefs and behaviors. He began to feel a sense of failure in his ability to maintain control over his behavior. Although experiencing a sense of exhilaration while fantasizing about the girl, Lee began to feel anxious, and the possibility of a relapse was imminent.

At this point in the relapse process, a number of events could occur. If Lee believed that he no longer had a problem with his sexually deviant behavior, the loss of control he was experiencing could be devastating. Feeling a sense of failure, his progression to actually reoffending would be high. However, if Lee was able to view his lapse in the context of a warning that he was in danger, he could remove himself from the situation and feel some success at having interrupted the chain of events that in all likelihood ultimately could have resulted in a new sexual offense.

If Lee chooses to exit the situation, the expectation is that Lee would view the lapse situation as an opportunity in which he did exercise self-management. Using his coping response of escape, and viewing the series of circumstances he created as steps leading to his potential relapse, Lee could begin to be more realistic in how he will deal with future occasions of high-risk behaviors. It would be important for Lee to take the next step of discussing in detail everything that occurred with his treatment group, probation officer, AA sponsor, and Nan.

Use of the relapse prevention model engages offenders in examining their own patterns of relapse. It allows both the offenders and the probation/parole officer to examine the chain of events that are put into place prior to relapse. It also provides the offenders with opportunities to intervene in their own relapse cycle, thus giving them tools to manage their own behaviors.

Development of the Supervision Network

The creation and use of a supervision network increases the accuracy and consistency of information pertaining to an offender's routine behaviors and activities in a given period of time. It also provides a more structured framework to the supervision process. In developing a supervision network, significant individuals in the offender's life are identified, with community supervision enhanced when the probation/parole officer maintains contacts with these individuals.

Meetings in the probation/parole office with offenders provide only a "snapshot" of offenders' activities; time is limited, and offenders may attempt to portray themselves and their situations in the best light possible. Offenders are often seemingly compliant, yet can be vigilant secret keepers. Use of a supervision network allows the probation/parole officer to interact routinely with individuals more familiar with the offenders and their day-to-day activities.

Professional Network

The professional network is comprised of individuals who have contact with sex offenders through their professional roles, such as law enforcement, correctional staff, social workers, therapists, school personnel, or health care workers.

However, some professionals may have difficulty with the concept of a supervision network that promotes the exchange of information regarding the offenders' risk. Some therapists, for instance, may feel their relationship with the offender will be compromised if they communicate with a probation/parole officer regarding their client's progress or lack of progress in treatment (see Questions for the Therapist, page 92). The therapist also may be hesitant to work with a limited confidentiality waiver (see waiver, page 131). Law enforcement and social service agencies are less likely to have this hesitation. In fact, many child protection services and law enforcement agencies have developed protocols to encourage the flow of information.

Nonprofessional Network

The nonprofessional network is comprised of individuals such as family members, employers, neighbors, friends, AA/NA sponsors, and landlords. Family members may encourage the changes offenders need to make and, therefore, have incentive in supporting the offenders by becoming part of the supervision network. Employers who value the offenders' abilities in the workplace and their efforts to live safely in the community also would be beneficial members of the supervision network. Generally, these individuals have routine contact with the offenders and see the offenders in their day-to-day activities.

Before including people in the supervision network, it is important to assess their appropriateness. Will their support allow them to look critically at offenders' behavior in the community, or will their support be designed to keep offenders in the community regardless of increased risk? To consider these individuals as part of the supervision network, ask some of the questions in the box on the next page.

People Appropriate for Supervision Network

- Do they believe the offender committed the offense?
- Are they knowledgeable about the offense dynamics? Do they know and recognize the offender's risk factors?
- Do they agree to not keep secret the offender's risky activities?
- Are they willing to speak with the probation/parole officer about the offender's activities?
- Is the probation/parole officer welcome to contact them or come to their home or place of business?

Not all persons in an offender's life will be appropriate or willing to be a part of the supervision network. Individuals who display anti-authority attitudes, who do not believe in the offender's guilt, or who support the offender in victim blaming will be inappropriate. Do not include individuals who strongly believe in the myths about sex offenders (such as, the victim must have wanted it because she did not fight back) and cannot be swayed from these beliefs. They probably will not be reliable judges of behavior that may be risky on the part of the offender. Although the work ethic is valued highly by our society, beware of the employer who values the offender's workaholic tendencies to the point of refusing to see them as risk factors. Workaholic tendencies often mask the offender's reluctance to address areas which have historically increased the offender's risk. Reviewing the previous example of Lee and Nan, the probation officer could have been aware earlier of Lee's increasing stressors and his inadequate coping responses if he or she were in regular contact with Nan.

Volunteer Network

Correctional volunteers can be an integral part of the network and can assist sex offenders' successful reintegration into the community as nonabusing citizens. For the offender who has reading and writing deficits, the volunteer may help the offender with homework assignments from the treatment group. For the offender who has spent many years in prison and no longer has a family support system, the volunteer may provide an invaluable role in helping that offender reintegrate back into the community. For the socially isolated sex offender, the volunteer could participate with the offender in appropriate leisure time activity.

Volunteers will need to receive training in the dynamics of sexual abuse and the relapse prevention model. Volunteers provide an important link between the professional and nonprofessional network. In Vermont, volunteers working with sex offenders meet monthly for peer support and advanced training.

Network Supervision

Identify members of the network in the case plan. Make it clear to the offender that information regarding risk will be shared among members of the supervision network. Give examples to the offender of what type of information may be exchanged among members of the professional, nonprofessional, and volunteer networks. For example, the probation/parole officer may ask the AA/NA sponsor about the offender's attendance at AA meetings. Sex offenders who decrease AA attendance may be placing their sobriety in jeopardy, therefore increasing their risk of engaging in high-risk behaviors.

Offenders will need to discuss their offenses and risk factors with those individuals in the supervision network. Offenders will be informed that the probation/parole officer will contact the network members to ensure that offenders have contacted them and have provided them with accurate information. This assists the probation/parole officer in assessing how knowledgeable and forthcoming offenders are about their risk factors and begins to tear down the walls of secrecy offenders have been so careful to construct.

The success of the supervision network is dependent on the willingness and cooperation of the individuals involved to share information as well as the reliability of the information they provide. In choosing network individuals, it is important to educate them in the relapse prevention model and to assure them that their sharing of information can enhance the ability of the offender to reside safely in the community. Network members must be informed about how sharing information regarding the offender will be used and with whom it will be shared.

An important aspect of educating network members, particularly the nonprofessional network unfamiliar with relapse prevention, is to define and provide concrete examples of risk factors and lapse behaviors. It is important to stress that lapses are normal, expected and, in fact, everyone at some point in his or her life has experienced them. They may be as simple an act as reaching for a candy bar after diligent dieting and exercising or sneaking a cigarette after vowing to quit. However, with the sex offender, the stakes are higher; a lapse that is not addressed sufficiently can set the stage for reoffense. A pedophile who walks his dog by the elementary school playground is engaging in high-risk behavior. Taken by itself, walking a dog appears to be an innocent enough gesture, but for offenders who experience arousal to preadolescent children, a walk by a schoolyard is a lapse and places them in a high-risk situation.

Sharing risk factors and lapses with the probation/parole officer does not mean offenders will be remanded to jail or prison. However, it does mean that offenders will need to reexamine their decision-making processes, high-risk behaviors, and other events that may be occurring in their life. Refusal to do so by offenders potentially could result in removal from the community, depending upon the severity of the lapse. In not addressing lapse behavior, offenders increase their risk and thus pose a danger to the community.

It is incumbent on the probation/parole officer, at this point, to take steps to reduce the opportunities for the offender to commit yet another criminal act by increasing risk control and risk management. However, with training in successful problem solving, offenders will gain confidence in their ability to manage their behavior and be prepared when a lapse reoccurs. Both the probation/parole officer and therapist can assist in the process.

The sharing of information needs to happen with some immediacy. Rather than having network members evaluate the seriousness of the information before reporting it, they must be encouraged to share the information in a timely manner. Sharing the information early on may reduce the likelihood of the offender moving through the relapse chain. Although offenders may not agree with this view initially, successful management of lapses may increase their sense of control over their behaviors and their trust in the network.

Use of Surveillance

Typically, monitoring offenders has been carried out by probation/parole officers responsible for all aspects of sex-offender supervision. However, with the ever increasing volume of high-risk offenders, shrinking resources, and the use of specialized caseloads, many jurisdictions use surveillance officers in addition to probation/parole officers to better monitor offenders in the community.

Historically, surveillance officers have played a law-enforcement role, monitoring offender activities, using powers of arrest, conducting urinalysis and alcosensor testing, and making residence checks. The quality of supervision increases, however, when surveillance officers are included as part of the supervision team. Their observations become part of the larger context of information on the sex offender.

To provide sex offenders with effective supervision, the surveillance officer must receive specialized training on sex offender profiles, the nature of sexually deviant behavior, and the relapse prevention model. The officer's review of each offense, court-imposed conditions, and terms of the offenders' sentences will provide a basis for supervision. The surveillance officer should have information about victim type, use of drugs and/or alcohol, how the offender gained access to the victim, offense history, or other types of sexually deviant behavior. Familiarity with the offender's employment, residence, and supervision network also will be important.

Surveillance officers should be looking for information that not only indicates risky behaviors but offenders' success in monitoring their behaviors, as well. They should report changes in the offenders' routines or activities as well as conversations that reveal new information. Officers who develop rapport and are able to converse comfortably with sex offenders about personal issues enhance the quality of supervision. Supervision of sex offenders is a little like putting a puzzle together. Small pieces of information taken alone have little significance. However, when the pieces are put together, the picture that emerges often provides important information regarding the offenders' activities. These reviews are effectively done in collaboration with the probation/parole officer who will fill in information gaps regarding state of denial, level of compliance with court-imposed conditions, and other types of general information.

> Paul, thirty, a convicted child molester, lived alone. As a child he was diagnosed as developmentally disabled and lived between family and institutions until four years ago. Aside from working as a volunteer at a local pet shelter, Paul spent much of his free time alone. During a field check, the surveillance officer noted that Paul had moved a chair by a window allowing him to watch activity on the street outside and reported this to Paul's parole officer. Paul's parole officer, in turn, reported that at her last meeting with Paul, he had talked about feeling lonely and admitted he had fantasized about having a child visit him. The therapist had also reported Paul talking in therapy about his loneliness. It was decided that the surveillance officer would drive by Paul's home at various times of the day to see what Paul was watching out his window.
>
> During an afternoon check, the surveillance officer noted a group of youngsters gathering at the corner across the street from Paul's apartment. The officer immediately parked his car and went to Paul's room. Paul invited him in, and the officer noted that Paul had been sitting in the chair as indicated by a soda and chips by the chair. Conversation with Paul revealed that children passed by his house after school and stopped on occasion at the corner. Paul acknowledged fantasizing about the children. He said he was thinking about going to the corner sometime and maybe the children would let him talk with them.
>
> It was clear to the officer that Paul was engaging in high-risk behavior through his continued observation of the children. As part of the intervention plan formulated by the supervision team, Paul's hours at the pet shelter were changed from mornings to afternoons so Paul would be at work when school got out. Paul was able to move to a back apartment which had recently become vacant, and Paul's sense of loneliness became a focus in treatment.

In this case, the surveillance officer was able to provide information that showed Paul at risk. Had Paul continued in his cycle, reoffense was a distinct possibility. The team composed of the surveillance officer, therapist, parole officer, and the mental health case manager (who worked individually with Paul on issues of his developmental disability) were able to interrupt the relapse cycle and thus diminished the possibility of a reoffense in this case.

Case Planning

The case planning process forms the basis for sex-offender supervision. The probation and parole officer develops it in conjunction with the offender at the onset of supervision. It reflects all the available and relevant information regarding the offender, including the special conditions of probation or parole. This is not to imply that offenders determine how they will be supervised, rather, the most effective case plans are developed with full awareness and understanding on the part of the offenders regarding responsibilities during the duration of supervision. The overall case manager of the sex offender case is the probation/parole officer who has the responsibility of directing the offender's activities while under supervision. The presentence investigation report is the operative time to set the groundwork for development of the initial case plan and to recommend the special conditions necessary for effective supervision.

The case plan is driven by quality and verifiable information. The initial case plan will reflect information available at the time the offender is beginning community supervision. As more information about the offender becomes available and as the offender's level of risk changes, so will elements of the case plan. During the life of supervision, the case plan will reflect information that either supports the direction of the initial case plan or requires the use of a different approach.

Agencies will have differing formats for case plans. Some will be elaborate using terms and technology specific to that agency; others will be simple and similar to a contract. Case plans that clearly spell out the offender's responsibilities will eliminate confusion later on during supervision. An additional benefit of a comprehensive case plan is that the surveillance officer or interim supervising officer can use it as a tool.

At a minimum, the case plan should contain the following elements:

- biographical data (offender name, date of birth, address, employment)
- type of offense
- level of risk
- risk factors
- how and when the offender is to fulfill responsibilities
- information instructing the offender how supervision will be structured and monitored
- a signature/date line indicating the offenders' participation in the case-planning process

Probation and parole agencies may have different policies about when initial case planning must occur. A common time frame is thirty days from sentencing. This provides an opportunity to assess the offender's initial response to court or parole board conditions while still completing the case-planning process in a timely manner. Be aware of your agency's policy to assist in information gathering.

Writing the Case Plan

Details of offense: To begin preparation for case planning, all relevant sources of information, such as police report, offender statement, and victim statement need to be gathered and reviewed. Look for themes to indicate if the offender has an established pattern of high-risk behaviors.

Additional information sources: If a presentence investigation report has not been completed, obtain the prior conviction record, history of probation/parole supervision, past treatment history, and response to treatment. This is particularly relevant with past sex-offender treatment but would extend to any type of treatment. For example, if the offender has been remanded to substance abuse treatment facilities in the past but left the program prior to completion of treatment, this may indicate denial regarding substance abuse, an unwillingness to follow rules and regulations, or poor follow-through on stated goals. The case manager should conduct research to discover whether the offender has accessed services from other agencies. If the family of the offender is being monitored by social services for other issues such as intrafamilial violence, this fact should be included in the case-planning process. Returning the offender to a chaotic situation could create a high-risk situation for reoffense. For further information, review Chapter 1, on personal history.

Offender interview: Have offenders detail their offense and compare it with the police statement or the offenders' previous statements. Offenders may add or delete details once sentencing has occurred. Discuss the offenders' history of supervision or treatment. Do the offenders deny any type of difficulties, blame their conviction on extraneous sources, or are they noncompliant in meeting responsibilities? Also, assess offenders' level of comprehension about their responsibilities. Case planning will differ with offenders who have limited abilities and skills, from offenders who demonstrate strong criminal attitudes and from offenders who in some areas of their life are positive, contributing members of the community. This is not to say that one group deserves privileges or exceptions. Rather, case plans must be specific to the individual offender and not generic to the offense. For information, review Chapter 1, interview format for offense history.

Court- or parole board-imposed conditions: Often conditions imposed by courts or parole boards are generic and not specific to individual crimes or offenders. Common examples of such conditions refer to offenders not having any contact with their victim(s), not purchasing or consuming alcoholic beverages, submitting to alcosensor or urinalysis testing, not possessing firearms or dangerous weapons, not being convicted (or in some cases not being charged) with new criminal offenses, and restrictions on out-of-state travel.

Many of these probation/parole conditions simply can be transferred to the case plan if they are specific enough in their intent. For example, a condition requiring an offender to pay $100 monthly in fines or restitution until $1,000 is paid is relatively straightforward. The imposed condition lists the total amount, the payment schedule, and the monthly amount. Not all imposed conditions are this clear. Many will require explanations of how the condition is to be met. This is particularly true with conditions for sex offenders. Conditions that appear straightforward may actually need to be individualized to the sex offender. Note the condition prohibiting the purchase and/or consumption of alcohol if deemed appropriate by the probation officer.

> Jack, twenty-seven, was convicted of sexual assault on a minor. He was able to continue employment with a drafting firm and had a reasonably good work record. He had demonstrated responsibility in setting up his outpatient counseling as a sex offender and was not assessed as having problems with drugs or alcohol. The probation officer imposed a condition in the case plan prohibiting Jack from purchasing, possessing, and/or consuming alcoholic beverages. This was done with full knowledge on the part of the officer that Jack was not a substance abuser.

The probation officer in preparation for writing the case plan had accessed all the necessary information available. He noted in the prior criminal record a charge of furnishing malt beverages to a minor in which Jack received a fine. He further learned from reading the presentence investigation report that Jack had been dismissed from a position with the local parks department when he was in college because of fraternizing with the youth and neglecting his duties as a lifeguard. Jack's recent offense was for fondling an eleven-year-old boy. Two other charges involving the same victim were dismissed in exchange for a guilty plea. In each of the allegations and the criminal conviction, Jack used alcohol as a way to lure the boy. Purchasing beer for the boy was used as part of the "grooming process."

Consider how the imposition of a specialized condition will impact on the offender and either become a deterrent or enable the offender to engage in high-risk behaviors. For example, if the incest offender is allowed supervised visitation with his children, including his victim, by the court or parole board order, be specific about how that visitation is to occur, who is to chaperone the visit and how the officer will receive feedback on the visit from the chaperone. Apply this standard to all the court- or parole board-imposed conditions.

Consider available resources: Evaluate the resources available in providing comprehensive supervision of the sex offender. Many jurisdictions manage their populations according to risk and provide resources accordingly, such as intensive supervision, surveillance officers, and /or electronic monitoring. It is not uncommon for other officers in the agency to be familiar with the offender or have other family members under supervision. Many probation and parole officers have long correctional memories and may recall particular behaviors that were precursors to high-risk activities.

> Raoul was on parole for the sexual assault of a woman. His partner, Deborah, was being supervised for a series of bad checks. Deborah came into the office with a blackened eye, refused to divulge what happened, and offered no comment when asked if Raoul had hit her. Deborah's probation officer informed Raoul's officer of the office visit and her suspicion regarding domestic violence in the home. With this information, Raoul's officer increased home visits and Deborah's officer worked with Deborah on domestic violence issues. Two weeks later, Deborah told her probation officer that Raoul had blackened her eye although she also stated that he had never hit her before. Both officers worked with a women's advocate from the local shelter to create a safety plan for Deborah. Raoul was placed in a domestic violence program in addition to the sex-offender treatment.

The probation/parole officer who works in collaboration with the community resources will enhance the quality of supervision. This information should be stated on the case plan and shared with the offender if the information does not involve risk to others. It is important that the offender understands that supervision will be far reaching, providing fewer opportunities for the offender to avoid responsibility. Conversely, for the offender who takes responsibility seriously, the breadth of the supervision network also provides more opportunities for honest feedback, support, and encouragement for the offender, where appropriate.

Policy considerations: Each local agency may have specific policy and practice on case planning. Some of those practices may be related to the specific form used, how frequently particular categories of offenders must report to their probation/parole officer, how frequently offenders must be seen in the community, or specific conditions automatically applied to types of offenders such as sex offenders. Using information provided in this section blended with agency practice will enhance the case-planning process.

Using the Case Plan

Supervising according to the case plan: As indicated earlier, the probation/parole officer writes the case plan along with input from the offender. The officer is designated as the case manager, overseeing the supervision of the offender and monitoring the offender's response to the conditions imposed on the case plan. However, the case plan can be used by other staff who provide supervision services. For example, if the surveillance officer is providing field checks, that officer will need to have access to the case plan to learn the areas of risk and to understand the scope of the offender's supervision.

For those agencies that use team supervision for sex offenders, the case plan is an invaluable tool. The team not only pulls together those charged with supervision of the offender, but is a forum for exchange of information. The case plan is useful to guide discussion on the offender and provide a focus in team meetings for gaining a comprehensive picture of the offender's activities. For example, if the team is discussing an offender who is a year into sex-offender treatment and recently began supervised visitation with his children, the case plan encourages discussion about risk in relation to the visits but also will focus on other issues such as employment, which may be relevant to the current case. If the team learns that the offender has been missing time at work, this behavior may have significant relevance to the offender's start-up of visitation with his children. Use of the case plan encourages comprehensive discussion on the offender's supervision.

Maintaining the case plan: Maintenance of the case plan is an ongoing task which must be managed by the probation/parole officer. Because the case plan is not intended to be a fixed document, changes will occur in the case plan as new information is discovered, such as when the offender is making positive strides, or when the offender is displaying high-risk behavior. As certain elements of the case plan are completed, the case manager should note this information in the case plan. For example, if the offender was required to undergo a substance abuse assessment, the results of the assessment should be noted in the file and removed from the case plan as an ongoing obligation. This is particularly important if the case is handled by an interim probation/parole officer, or if there should be further court proceedings. It would be embarrassing to hold an offender accountable to an item in the case plan that was already completed. Individual agencies have varying policies on the frequency of case plan review. At the very least, it is important that case plans be reviewed monthly to keep the plan current and to include additional relevant information in a timely manner.

The case plan is meant to be a useful document, updated when chan
created in a format that any staff person involved in the offender's super
For example, it should be clear to the officer reviewing the case plan th... a rapist not
secure employment as a cab driver or any position that allows him access to homes.
These jobs would allow him the opportunity to become familiar with women's residences. Elements of the case plan are designed to be instructive with a level of detail
helpful to both staff and the offender. The case plan is intended to be an instructive
guide and a beneficial tool that provide the basis for the offender's supervision.

Ongoing Supervision

Developing a case plan, identifying and educating the supervision network, and
referring the offender to treatment may take two weeks to two months, depending
on the probation/parole officer's workload, availability of specialized treatment, and
department practice and policy.

Throughout the process of setting up the supervision framework, the proba-
tion/parole officer should make sure offenders are clear about their responsibilities.
Offenders must be prepared to discuss details of their offense and high-risk behaviors, as well as potential risk situations that may occur on a day-to-day basis. For
example, in accounting for their leisure time, offenders should inform their proba-
tion/parole officers of any reduction in their work hours. Unaccounted or unplanned
leisure time may provide offenders opportunities to engage in deviant behavior. In
discussing risk, offenders should be engaging in problem solving and development of
strategies to cope with high-risk situations.

At the beginning of supervision, place emphasis on supervision and surveillance
during this time. Make clear to the offenders that reports regarding risky or questionable activities are always best if they come from the offenders. Reports of lapse
behavior will not necessarily result in legal sanctions. What will be evaluated is
whether offenders are taking responsibility, developing coping strategies, and carrying through on their plan to correct lapses.

Establish rapport to encourage offenders to talk freely about their activities
without feeling fearful, intimidated, or threatened. The probation/parole officer
should do whatever is possible to ensure that during office visits there is a confidential space for offenders to privately discuss their sexually deviant behaviors.

Dealing with Lapse Behavior

A lapse is an emotion, fantasy, thought, or behavior that is part of the offender's
relapse pattern. Lapses with sex offenders are not unusual and should be anticipated.
Lapses occur when an offender fails to monitor warning signs or fails to address

high-risk situations. The lapse behavior that goes "unchecked" can have disastrous results, culminating perhaps in the commission of a new offense. Lapses occur when offenders:

- fail to develop coping skills for high-risk factors
- continue to expose themselves to high-risk situations
- fail to adequately deal with conflict
- experience difficulty in maintaining interpersonal relationships with family, spouse, and friends
- experience difficulty in dealing with emotional feelings such as anger, anxiety, and depression

Lapse behavior can cover a wide range of actions and attitudes. Lapses will be individual to the offender and to the type of deviant behaviors in which the offender has engaged. Lapse behaviors identified during the initial period of supervision may change as time goes on and new areas of risk may be identified. Some lapses will be part of the specialized conditions of probation or parole. The following are common examples of lapses for a sex offender: engaging in deviant fantasy, purchasing pornography, using alcohol, being alone with a child, or not resolving feelings of anger.

The probation/parole officer must realize that lapse behavior is expected and when discovered should be dealt with immediately. It is best when offenders share the information about lapses with the probation/parole officer and therapist. However, this may not happen, and the behavior may be disclosed by someone in the supervision network.

Evaluating the Lapse

When the probation/parole officer discovers the offender has engaged in lapse behavior, he or she must consider the following:

(1) How serious is the lapse behavior?
(2) What level of responsibility is the offender taking for the lapse behavior?
(3) Has the offender developed a plan to address the lapse behavior?

The following is an example of an offender engaged in a lapse who reported it both in treatment and to his probation officer.

> Walter, twenty-eight, was on probation for exhibitionism. He was attending college part-time and frequently put off his assignments until the last minute. This became a problem when one of his regular assignments was to submit a typewritten paper on Monday mornings. Because of putting off tasks until the last moment, Walter was often at

the school Sunday evenings typing his paper. After a few weeks, Walter reported to his therapist that he was having sexual fantasies about one of the female students who was also at school on Sunday evenings. The previous Sunday, Walter became so anxious about the urge to expose himself that he left the classroom, forgetting his coat.

Walter discussed the lapse in his treatment group. He admitted that he deliberately might be planning the last-minute rush to complete the assignment. Walter decided, with the group's help, that he needed to plan his week more efficiently. The weekly typewritten assignment was to be completed no later than Friday, rather than leaving it to the last minute. Walter agreed to no longer do homework assignments at the school library unless he was with a male friend who knew of his offense and risk factors.

Walter shared all of this information with his probation officer. The probation officer determined that Walter had created a high-risk situation for himself and had experienced a lapse by fantasizing about the female student at the school. Walter, however, had shared this information in a timely manner with the appropriate individuals, had taken full responsibility for the lapse behavior, and had identified a solution to the problem on which he acted. In this particular situation, Walter had successfully dealt with a lapse and experienced a feeling of success at having interrupted his relapse pattern.

Not all situations are this straightforward. Note the following situation which illustrates the process and importance of networking.

Ken, twenty-eight, was on probation for molesting his stepson. On a routine drive through Ken's neighborhood, the probation officer noted a male adolescent mowing the lawn at Ken's home. The probation officer found Ken in his basement working on a project. When confronted about the boy mowing his lawn, Ken said his landlord must have hired the boy. Ken further stated he was not acquainted with the boy.

The probation officer spoke with Ken for some time going over his risk factors while emphasizing that the boy mowing the lawn presented a dangerous situation for Ken. Despite being reminded of his risk factors, Ken continued to state he was not aware the boy was there. The probation officer then spoke to the boy who said his mother had dropped him off to mow the lawn and that he had no contact with Ken. The probation officer offered to give the boy a ride home to remove him from the situation. Ironically, the boy declined the offer saying he wasn't to ride with strangers and left on his own.

ıe probation officer had a bad feeling about the situation, given
.'s history, lackluster participation in therapy, and the nonchalant
. y he regarded the lawnmowing incident. Unable to reach the boy's
mother, the probation officer made a number of calls to Ken's landlord
(who lived out of state), his employer, and members of Ken's extended
family, inquiring about their assessment of Ken's current situation.
Subsequent meetings with Ken focused on lapse behaviors and his failure to adequately address a high-risk situation.

While Ken continued to refuse to acknowledge the seriousness of the
lawnmowing incident, the probation officer received a phone call from
a network member revealing Ken had recently attended a family gathering where children were present. This was clearly a violation of Ken's
probation and an indication that Ken was intentionally involved in
high-risk activities. The probation officer also learned that the young
man mowing Ken's lawn had had this job all summer and had received
little gifts from Ken over the past few months. Ken, subsequently, had
his probation revoked and served the underlying sentence.

In these situations, the probation officer applied the relapse prevention model to
both provide opportunities for the offender to apply internal controls to his behaviors and reduce the probability of a reoffense, with an externally controlled response
as a consequence for failure to do so. In each situation, the lapse behavior was individual to the offender's relapse pattern. Interrupting the pattern can be as straightforward as the offender recognizing the high-risk behavior and successfully
intervening. The use of a coordinated response to interrupt the relapse pattern using
increased external controls (supervision, contact with the supervision network) also
can be applied. Clearly, lapses must be identified and successfully addressed before
they snowball into new, sexually aggressive acts.

Offenders in Denial

The first point of intervention with offenders in denial is during the presentence
investigation process. However, there always will be offenders who remain in denial
and receive probationary sentences. There also will be sex offenders paroled who are
in denial and who have received no treatment during their incarceration. Sex offenders in denial who live in the community pose an increased risk. It is difficult for the
probation/parole officer to monitor offenders' daily activities, particularly with
offenders who may be making no attempt to curtail their deviant activities.

Generally, at the beginning of supervision, what is known about the sex
offender's deviant behavior is the "tip of the iceberg." This makes supervision of sex

offenders challenging at best. With the dynamics that are present with an offender in denial, effective supervision becomes not only a challenge but involves both comprehensive monitoring and detective work. It is helpful to be familiar with how offenders present their denial when formulating treatment and supervision strategies (see Forms of Denial, page 11).

The most obvious example of denial is the offender who is in total, abject denial that the offense ever occurred. If offenders have been incarcerated for a number of years, their denial may be even more entrenched.

Similar, and equally serious, are offenders who take absolutely no responsibility and blame the victims, often in a hostile manner. These offenders not only are in denial around their sexually deviant activities, but also may challenge any attempts to get them to conform their behavior to socially accepted standards. These are the offenders who may deny knowing the victim was only fourteen or claim the rape was consenting and the woman is lying to save her reputation. These offenders may have prior convictions, not always for sex offenses, or have failed previously under probation or parole supervision. They rarely have engaged in any type of treatment and have a questionable work history. They live by their own code and see nothing wrong with themselves. Often, these offenders are found inappropriate for community treatment.

Other offenders, equally difficult to supervise, are those who may be appropriate for community treatment but who exhibit forms of denial that make supervision more difficult. For example, there are offenders who maintain the offense just happened without acknowledging any element of planning. These offenders are not denying that an offense was committed, but they are indicating an unwillingness to look at the elements leading up to commission of the offense. By refusing to examine precursors to their offense, offenders also are not allowing themselves to develop strategies to intervene in high-risk behaviors. Another example is offenders who admit the offense occurred, but are adamant in stating that it will never happen again. They may believe that having apologized to the victim or accepting responsibility for "that one incident" may preclude them from having to engage in treatment or having to be closely supervised. Other examples include offenders who stop drinking or return to their faith. They are placing the responsibility of change on extraneous sources. In refusing to acknowledge the possibility of relapse, they may "test" themselves in high-risk situations, placing unsuspecting potential victims at risk.

All of these examples portray sex offenders who present additional risk to the community by their unwillingness to recognize and/or intervene in their own deviant patterns. Probation/parole officers faced with supervising these individuals can adopt a number of strategies and techniques to address their increased level of risk. The first step is to set the framework for supervision.

Supervision means not only monitoring offenders' activities but engaging offenders in the process of change. As starters, officers should use techniques outlined in the presentence section to address denial with offenders. Reviewing the police affidavit and victim's statement with offenders and having offenders recount the offense with continued appropriate probing by the officer is important. Using the relapse prevention model is an effective technique, particularly when combining it with situations offenders are familiar with and may be less hesitant to discuss. Relating the model to weight loss, alcohol abuse, or cessation of smoking may be a less threatening way for offenders to draw some correlations. Reminding offenders that they have already been adjudicated by the court is important and that openly discussing their deviant patterns will not change their sentence, while refusing to acknowledge responsibility or cope appropriately with lapses will ultimately result in a return to court.

Some treatment programs have instituted groups specifically for offenders who are in denial of their offense. These groups are time limited and psychoeducational in their focus. Those offenders who begin to take responsibility and initiate a change in examining their offense patterns are referred to a regular sex-offender group. This referral will begin their compliance with their special condition to engage in sex-offender treatment. Offenders who remain steadfast in their denial at the end of the time-limited group will be returned to court or the parole board on a violation. In the request for revocation, the officer is able to demonstrate what efforts have been made to work with the offender in acknowledging deviant behavior and what the response of the offender has been. The court or parole board is able to see the attempts made to work with the offender and what level of risk the offender continues to pose, and to base a subsequent decision on these areas.

Another option therapists use for offenders in denial is to have them participate in a regular treatment group for a time-limited trial basis. The offenders can experience first hand what treatment will involve and associate with sex offenders who are addressing their sexually deviant problems. The group members also may have success in breaking through the offenders' denial.

Those offenders who are denying the planning or denying the difficulty of change usually are appropriate for community treatment but create challenges for the officer during supervision. These offenders may appear successful in their professions, within their community and family. The skills needed to advance in society are often the very same skills that allow the offenders to practice their deviant behaviors undetected. The probation/parole officer or any individuals working professionally with offenders must be vigilant in avoiding any collusion with the offenders. Although collusion is a strong word, many of these offenders do not fit the stereotype and subtly begin to convince the individuals working with them that they are not really "sex offenders." For example,

Ted, a successful restaurant owner, was active in community activities, was always the first one called to pitch in for charity events, and had friends in common with the probation officer. Although the officer had found it difficult to accept the fact that Ted could really be guilty of the charges, she also was a well-trained officer with experience in working with such offenders. In working with the offender, she concentrated on the police report and the statements made by the victims, and she began to develop a list of risk factors with Ted. She was thorough and cautious in her interviews with him. She began to identify holes in Ted's version of the offense. Any attempt by Ted to derail the interview was immediately curtailed by the officer who would bring the discussion back to the offense.

For those offenders who remain in denial, increased supervision is required. Team supervision is recommended to increase the quality of offender monitoring. With an unwillingness on the part of the offender to begin to address deviant sexual behavior, external controls must be implemented to enhance community safety. Offenders must be held strictly accountable to conditions on the probation/parole agreement as well as that of the case plan. Consequences for failure to abide by the conditions should be spelled out. It is equally important that there be action behind the statements.

If an offender has a condition of abstinence from substance use, the officer must periodically alcosensor or urine test the offender. If the offender tests positive, there must be a sanction. Officers must make contact with collateral contacts in the offender's network. Officers must contact the employer to verify if the offender remains in good standing at work and monitor the offender's participation in other types of treatment. The officer must make regular home visits to assess any changes or areas that may indicate potential risk. These tasks should occur routinely in the supervision of all sex offenders, yet they take on a heightened level of importance with the offender who refuses to practice any internal controls on behavior.

The use of teams increases the "eyes and ears" of supervision and the quantity and quality of information. The increased level of supervision must not be mistaken for an opportunity to merely catch the offender. Intensifying supervision increases accountability of offenders and presents additional opportunities to assess the level of risk they pose to the community. When offenders' behaviors indicate they pose risks to the community, there must be a system of graduated sanctions for such behavior. Offenders who are allowed to continue living in the community without sanctions for inappropriate behavior take this as a sign that their behavior is condoned.

Well-trained correctional professionals know that each offender is unique and that supervision and case planning must be specific to that offender's risks. Community safety must be of primary importance. Within your state's statutes and your department's policies, procedures, and practices, offenders must be given the opportunity to change and be encouraged in that process. This is important as the majority of offenders eventually are released back into the community. However, for those offenders who continuously demonstrate a refusal to exert any kind of internal control and positive change toward their deviant behavior, implementation of increased external controls must be exercised. These external controls include intensive supervision, electronic monitoring, and/or surveillance as well as the ultimate external control of incapacitation.

Transition from Incarcerative Program to Community Supervision

For those offenders who have participated in treatment in an incarcerative setting, transition from the correctional institution to parole supervision requires detailed planning and coordination. Transition to the community is fertile ground for high-risk behavior, even for those sex offenders who are essentially prosocial and skilled in day-to-day life management. For offenders who were incarcerated at an early age or have spent a significant amount of time in a prison setting, transition to the community can be overwhelming and unfamiliar. Some of these offenders have never held a job, taken a bus, paid bills, or made a doctor's appointment.

For offenders who have a history of criminal behavior, and have not yet practiced prosocial behaviors in the community, the transition can be particularly difficult. These offenders may be resistant to acknowledging how few skills they actually have in such simple tasks as buying groceries and cooking a meal. Saving face is more important. One offender who had terminated a long-term relationship was washing his clothes for the first time in a laundromat. He put too much soap in the machine and the machine overflowed with soap pouring onto the floor. The offender watched with shock as the manager came up to the machine asking whose clothes they were. Other people in the laundromat began to look around to see who had made this mistake. The offender quietly and quickly left the laundromat never to return. He chose to spend his next paycheck on buying new clothes rather then admit his mistake to the manager of the laundromat.

An effective transition plan to the community requires:

(1) Identification of appropriate residence, employment, and/or education
(2) Identification and education of the supervision network (professional, non-professional and volunteers)
(3) A gradual reentry plan

1. Residence, employment, and/or education

This is a critical area in initiating the reintegration process, particularly if a previously held job or residence is no longer appropriate. For the pedophile, a residence where children are present or a job which places him in proximity to children is unsuitable. For the rapist, a job or residence where alcohol is consumed or where individuals are hostile toward law enforcement is not appropriate.

Often, the process of identifying appropriate placements is time consuming and a process of elimination may need to occur before a suitable environment is developed. This process takes time and should be initiated with significant lead time prior to the proposed release date.

> Mark, convicted of rape, came from a family well known to law enforcement. Many members of Mark's family had criminal convictions. There were children in the home, and his ailing father continued to consume alcohol. There was little privacy and a great deal of tension in the home. Mark's parents were eager for him to return to assist in supporting the family. During his incarceration, Mark had actively participated in sex-offender treatment and identified situations which contributed to his high-risk behavior. In planning for his transition, Mark acknowledged a return to his family home at this time would be counterproductive, perhaps even dangerous, and he reluctantly began to consider alternate solutions.
>
> Mark required a drug- and alcohol-free residence in which the other individuals living there were fully informed of his offense and were supportive of his efforts at maintaining employment, treatment, and financial responsibilities. It was important that Mark's efforts to effectively manage his behavior were supported.
>
> During the process, Mark was rejected by a substance-abuse halfway house due to his conviction as a sex offender. He considered and decided against residence with an acquaintance who believed Mark's victim was asking for it. He turned down an employment situation in which he would be the sole caregiver for a disabled elderly man. Mark eventually decided to reside with his married sister and brother-in-law who had distanced themselves from the family. Mark noted that his previous relationship with his brother-in-law had been strained but acknowledged his previous lifestyle was a major cause.

In this example, Mark worked with treatment and parole staff to identify and secure an appropriate residence. Options were discussed, evaluated, and discarded when necessary. In working with the team, Mark learned that such decisions were not arbitrary and increased his understanding of what was expected of him on community release.

Once residence, employment, and/or education have been determined, it is necessary not only to provide information but to educate as well. It is not enough for the employer to know that the offender has been convicted of a sex offense, it is also important that he or she understand why certain restrictions need to be put in place. The employer at the county public works department should understand why the offender, convicted of child molestation, must not be used as a school crossing guard if the need suddenly should occur. Establishing these boundaries early on encourages the offender to anticipate and negotiate high-risk situations as they occur.

2. Supervision network

Prior to the offenders moving to community-based settings, the supervision network should be established. This is initiated by identifying the supervision network members (both professional and nonprofessional) and having offenders share information regarding their offense and risk factors with them. With professional network members, the offender must be informed as to the type of information the network will receive from the incarcerative program. Offenders also must know who their parole officer is, what contact the social service worker may have with them or their family, what law enforcement agencies have been notified regarding their release, and who their outpatient therapist will be. Appropriate documentation should be released to these parties for purposes of forming a better understanding of the offender and relapse patterns. Types of information to be shared would be conditions of release which spell out the court or parole board conditions, the offense affidavit, risk factors, and the offender's relapse prevention plan.

The offender must be clear on expectations regarding reporting, treatment, and other requirements standard for parolees. Where possible, it is recommended that the parole officer meet with the offender prior to community transition. This meeting would be the beginning of the case planning process (see Case Planning, page 44). The ideal situation is for the parole officer, offender, and incarcerative treatment team to meet and exchange information in a group format. A conference call is less desirable but a viable alternative. This cuts down on secrecy, minimization, or manipulativeness the offender may try with the parole officer once out in the community.

With the nonprofessional network, a group meeting is equally important. With either the parole officer or staff from the incarcerative program facilitating, the offender would outline the details of his offense, his risk factors and his coping strategies to his network. The network members could ask questions and the facilitator would ensure that all pertinent information was disclosed by the offender.

These meetings serve as an opportunity to pull together the parole officer, the support network and the offender in the transition process. This is an additional opportunity to evaluate the offender's transition plan, provide feedback and support, and develop alternatives. It is also an avenue for the offenders to become familiar offender would outline the details of his offense, his risk factors and his coping strategies to his network. The network members could ask questions and the facilitator would ensure that all pertinent information was disclosed by the offender.

These meetings serve as an opportunity to pull together the parole officer, the support network and the offender in the transition process. This is an additional opportunity to evaluate the offender's transition plan, provide feedback and support, and develop alternatives. It is also an avenue for the offenders to become familiar with the supervision network and be assured that they will be positively supported if they use the skills they learned in treatment.

3. Reentry plan

Transition from an incarcerative to a community-based setting is best accomplished gradually, allowing the offenders to practice skills while being closely monitored. Ideally, the offenders will receive limited furloughs from the correctional facility to initiate the employment search, start outpatient treatment, and begin meeting with their parole officer. Offenders are fulfilling legal and treatment obligations and at the same time are beginning to get a feel of what it is like to be back in a community setting. Both offenders and case managers should expect that the release from incarceration will be met with stressful situations requiring forethought, planning, and the use of coping strategies on the part of the offenders. The ability to discuss areas of stress, receive feedback, employ coping strategies, and continue to address lapses, before final release onto parole, is ideal. This also provides the outpatient therapist the opportunity to evaluate the offenders' responses to potential areas of risk they may experience while in the community. If offenders are successful in using their coping strategies, activities can be expanded to include leisure activities or family visits as a continuation of the reintegration process.

Furloughing an offender to the community can take the form of short visits of a few hours to living in the community for specified periods of time. Some jurisdictions will place offenders in supportive living situations, such as halfway houses. In this status, offenders receive intensive supervision and can be remanded to a more secure setting if they choose not to intervene in high-risk activities.

In those jurisdictions where an offender is released directly into the community without a gradual reentry, it is important to begin parole under the most intensive supervision available including electronic monitoring, polygraphy, and intensive supervision. Supervision is then decreased incrementally relative to the offender's behavior and performance in the community. This is best assessed by the team working with the offender representing varying perspectives regarding the offender's response to supervision, treatment, and ability to live safely in a community setting.

Chapter 3

Confidentiality and Public Disclosure

For roughly a decade, states have been passing laws requiring sex offenders to register with a law enforcement agency or notify the community of their status as sex offenders. With minor variations, registration laws require convicted sex offenders to register with local law enforcement agencies on their release from prison or their placement on probation. The registration typically includes name, address, conviction, and a mandate to update with each change of address. Community notification requires that the public be notified of a sex offender's conviction and residence.

The issue of community notification is complex and controversial, with legal challenges both to the constitutionality of some public notification laws and to an individual's right to privacy. There has been extreme reaction in some communities after notification occurred. For example, a sex offender's residence was burned down in Oregon, and in New Jersey, a father and son went to the residence of a sex offender and assaulted the man they assumed to be a sex offender, assaulting the wrong man.

Furthermore, community notification laws vary from state to state. The profile of the sex offender may determine whether the community is notified and the responsibility for notifying the community may vary. For example, in New Jersey, all convicted sex offenders are subject to community notification, which is done by law enforcement, while in Louisiana, the offender is responsible for notifying the community.

The intent behind community notification is, of course, public safety, but concern has been expressed whether notification, in fact, does increase public safety. Critics say sex offenders will be undeterred, continuing to offend outside the notification area, or, because it is impossible to notify all potential victims, the community will suffer a false sense of security. Proponents of community notification, however, argue that community notification does act as a deterrent, giving parents more ability to protect their children, and furthermore, they argue that notification will enhance treatment compliance.

In May 1996, the United States Congress amended the Violent Crime Control and Law Enforcement Act of 1994 to require the release of relevant information to protect the public from sexually violent offenders. This federal law reinforces the state registration laws in mandating that law enforcement agencies shall release relevant information that is necessary to protect the public concerning those sex offenders who are required to register in their particular state. In August, 1996, President Clinton announced that the federal government would set up a national computer registry to track convicted sex offenders by linking up to an existing computer program that already collects state information.

Over and beyond the community notification laws, there are policies within each correctional department dealing with how and when to notify. A probation/parole officer faces a myriad of disclosure issues on a daily basis. This chapter will address the routine but vital considerations in the area of disclosure. For example, who should know about the sex offender's offense history, and when should they know it? How should this disclosure be made? How detailed should the released information be? Many correctional departments have clear mandates on the extent and type of disclosure required. Other departments, though, may be in the early stages of developing standards of disclosure in regard to sex offenders, which may leave their probation/parole officers feeling uncertain. Community notification laws also will drive how correctional departments respond to this issue. Being familiar with your states's registration and community notification is important. Liability issues, for both ethical and legal reasons, loom large in the life of the probation/parole officer.

Reporting Incidences of Child Sexual Abuse

Probation/parole officers are required to report any information that pertains to suspected incidence of child sexual or physical abuse, past or present. The law is clear and uncomplicated on this issue. The probation/parole officer should, at the onset of supervision and/or the presentence investigation, inform the offender of this law and his or her responsibility to report. Do not assume the offender knows the law. When discussing this mandate with the offender, it is important to discuss not only the need to protect a child from ongoing harm, but to provide the child with treatment once the disclosure has been made.

Duty to Warn

When there is an identified victim who is at risk from the offender, that potential victim must be warned. Therapists are also required to warn a potential victim if a victim is identifiable (*Tarasoff v. Regents of the University of California*, 1976). A likely example for a probation/parole officer is the child molester who proposes to live in a duplex with children next door.

If the offender is allowed to move into the duplex, those parents need to be aware of the offender's conviction and the special condition of probation/parole limiting the offender's access to minor children. The more difficult question, though, is how many houses with children should be informed when a sex offender moves into a neighborhood. Should it be two houses on either side, the entire block, or all homes within a three block radius? Of course, if the probation/parole officer has the authority (through conditions of probation/parole) to direct where a sex offender lives, he or she could prevent a child molester from residing in a neighborhood that is comprised predominantly of families with young children.

Disclosing to the Community

Using the supervision strategies outlined in this book, it is offenders' responsibility to notify people in their support network of their offense and risk factors. The probation/parole officer verifies that the disclosure has been true and complete and that he or she will be in regular contact with the network members who are also aware of the special conditions of probation/parole. A waiver of confidentiality should be signed by the offenders so the probation/parole officer can disclose information on an as-needed basis to support people in the network.

In regards to treatment, experienced sex-offender therapists will require the offenders to sign a limited waiver of confidentiality (see page 131) before agreeing to provide treatment. This waiver, in essence, allows the therapist to report the occurrence, or potential occurrence, of risky behavior to the appropriate authorities (including, of course, the probation/parole officer). Offenders have the ability to revoke the waiver at any time, but they are informed that treatment will be terminated without the waiver. If this occurs, the probation/parole officer would request a violation. The therapist also has offenders sign a treatment agreement outlining the conditions of treatment and the reporting agreement to the probation/parole officer of any violation of the treatment agreement (see pages 132–134). This treatment agreement allows the therapist to have open communication with the probation/parole officer.

The more perplexing issue, though, is the protection of community members outside offenders' support network or for those community members whose daily lives bring them into contact with sex offenders who may not be cooperating with treatment or supervision. Criminal convictions and special conditions of probation are a matter of public record and, therefore, disclosure of convictions and probation conditions by the probation officer should be no problem. However, check with your department as to their policy on this and whether community notification laws in your state dictate the disclosure. When determining what and to whom to disclose, it is helpful to make decisions based on the risk offenders may pose in a particular situation. If a team is involved, then, of course, disclosure decisions will be made by the team.

When only the probation/parole officer is establishing the link between certain community members and offenders, the officer has a duty to inform them of offenders' risk factors to allow community members to make an informed decision regarding contact with the offender, such as if the probation/parole officer were to make the job referral for the offender.

The special conditions of probation/parole can be critical in assisting the probation/parole officer in carrying out the necessary disclosures or in requiring changes in the offender's life that will protect the community. For example, consider an elementary school teacher on probation for sexually abusing girls. One of the special conditions may be that he not associate with minors without prior approval from the probation officer. Obviously, a teacher will come in contact with children on a daily basis, and with this special condition, the probation officer has the authority to require the offender to cease employment in that capacity and to find a job without contact with minor children.

Or take for example, the child molester who initiates a relationship with a woman with children. She needs to be aware of the offender's conviction, his risk factors, and his special conditions of probation or parole. Probation/parole conditions will assist in determining how to deal with this situation. If the special condition prevents the offender from socializing with women with minor children, then certainly the offender is in violation of his probation/parole. If the special condition only limits his association with minor children, the probation/parole officer still will be able to curtail his contact with the children although not with the mother. Disclosure provides the opportunity for community members to make educated decisions regarding their own contact with the offender.

Appropriate and timely disclosure to the community is key in supervising sex offenders, but educating the public is also critical. Notification without education can lead to extreme reactions that may be counterproductive for the community and prevent sex offenders who are sincere in changing their behaviors, to reintegrate with the community safely.

Liability

What are the liability issues in the supervision of a sex offender? What could be considered negligent supervision? What information, exactly, is a probation/parole officer allowed to disclose?

Be aware of differing policies regarding disclosure with adjunct mental health and substance-abuse treatment providers. For purposes of treatment efficacy, there must be collaboration between providers of ancillary treatment services. Offenders need to sign waivers of confidentiality for collaboration to occur. Substance-abuse treatment providers will be bound by separate policies to include mandatory federal guidelines (42, Part 2, *Code of Federal Regulations*).

To avoid issues of personal liability, find out what the policies are in your own department and adhere to them. Unfortunately, policies may not be current or reflect the community notification laws in your state. These policies need to be updated, both to provide officers with less legal peril and to safeguard the community.

If notification is inherent in the special conditions of probation/parole, then it is negligent not to notify. For example, a child molester who has a special condition that limits his access to minor children, may have a job that brings him into contact with children. The employer, in this situation, must be notified. This also allows the probation/parole officer to evaluate the appropriateness of the job.

Know and adhere to established policies on file maintenance. Department policy should dictate what information can be released, how it is to be released, and to whom. In some jurisdictions, there are reports that only can be released by the parole board or the court. Be aware of these distinctions and adhere to them. Consulting with team members or your supervisor lessens a probation/parole officer's sense of isolation and, furthermore, provides a safeguard against inadvertently breaching confidentiality regulations.

Finally, it is wise to record in the file how decisions are reached, what the plan is for disclosure, and how the disclosure plan will be followed through. Reoffenses are going to occur even with the most comprehensive supervision; the issue is, though, that the probation/parole officer act in a responsible manner in his or her supervision practices. Although there are many safety issues regarding sex offenders rejoining our communities, it is also important not to enable an atmosphere that ostracizes them and prevents them from having a safe reentry. In our experience, notification that also educates community members has reduced ostracism and has allowed for a safer reintegration.

Documentation

The ability to accurately review an offender's case depends on effective record keeping. This documentation benefits those working with the offender in providing an accurate and timely picture of the offender's treatment and supervision. Documentation serves a variety of purposes; however, exercise caution around a number of areas. What is the purpose in maintaining various types of documentation? Who is charged with maintaining documentation? How will information be used and who has access? How is information to be stored and disposed?

Documentation may be needed to satisfy a variety of areas. The box on the next page shows some of the areas to be considered when setting up record keeping and documentation of offender information.

(1) How is the offender meeting the court-imposed conditions and fulfilling requirements of probation? Does the file reflect when supervision meetings take place? Is there documentation on how and when the offender met the court-imposed conditions?

(2) What progress has occurred? How has the offender met the requirements of the case plan?

(3) Does the file reflect communication between the probation/parole officer and the treatment provider? Does it meet agency and statutory mandates?

(4) Is there documentation highlighting changes in the offender's status, such as custody changes, warning status in the treatment group, increased or decreased supervision?

Documentation should be succinct, informative, and professional in nature. A good rule to employ is that information contained in an offender's case file should be entered with the probability that it at some point will be subject to legal review. Some probation/parole officers have found that off-the-cuff opinions become public at court hearings. This may reflect bias and has no place in objectively documenting offender activities and interventions during the course of supervision.

Documentation forms the basis for review of an offender's period of supervision, as it details ongoing offender issues and the impact of interventions that have occurred during the course of supervision. Documentation should reflect ongoing assessment of the offender's treatment progress. Transition issues also must be documented as the offender moves to different levels of treatment and supervision, as well as to different probation/parole officers. It should be verifiable, objective, and able to withstand legal scrutiny. Documentation, although time consuming, is critical and forms the basis of the legal record. It should be used to inform, teach, evaluate, assess, and monitor offenders during their period of community supervision.

Probation/Parole Violations

Deciding if and when a violation should be brought is difficult and often tricky. Some situations demand revocation, such as the conviction of a new sexual offense. The conviction of a new nonsexual offense also requires attention. Examine the circumstances in which the violation occurred, such as criminal behavior that involves the use of substances, violence, or manipulation of another for personal or monetary gain.

When considering the seriousness of a technical violation, it is helpful to look at the offender's offense pattern, risk factors, and imposed conditions. Part of the relapse-prevention supervision strategy is to become aware of problems early on so they can be resolved without a violation being necessary. At the same time, depending on the offender's level of risk, a relatively minor infraction may require immediate court action.

The following situations warrant consideration:

- Contact with victim or potential victim
- Failure to reduce or avoid high-risk factors. For example, has the offender continuously failed to avoid situations that reinforce deviant fantasies?
- Failure to fully participate in mandated specialized treatment
- Evidence that the offender has used drugs and/or alcohol
- Failure to maintain a safe living environment
- Refusal to share information in treatment or with network members
- Has the offender revoked the limited confidentiality waiver?
- Have special conditions of probation been violated?

Assessing the seriousness of the technical violation is critical. Each infraction is not going to result in a violation. However, each infraction should be addressed directly, whether in the form of a warning, an increased level of supervision, or an issue to be addressed in treatment. The team approach is helpful in evaluating the level of risk and deciding on appropriate action (see Teamwork, page 113).

> Hugh, a convicted child molester, had been in treatment for four months. Although signing an agreement to pay $20 weekly for treatment, Hugh continuously failed to do so. Hugh came late to group, forgot his homework, failed to participate in group, and was generally noncompliant in the treatment process. During this period of time, Hugh was given a verbal warning about his behavior from the therapist which was documented. Hugh was given other opportunities to address the problems, both individually and in group, and this was again noted by the probation officer in the file. Hugh provided no explanation regarding his failure to fully participate in treatment and was subsequently given a written warning by the therapist, outlining the problems and potential consequences for continued poor participation and nonpayment. When no improvement was forthcoming, Hugh was returned to court for a technical probation violation.
>
> Despite the fact that there was no new criminal charge, the probation officer was concerned that Hugh was doing little to address his issues of sexual deviancy and was providing the group and therapist with no opportunity to gauge his level of responsibility for his criminal behavior or what, if any, positive changes were occurring. With Hugh's lax view of his responsibilities, the probation officer was concerned about the level of risk Hugh was presenting in the community.
>
> During the violation hearing, the defense attorney argued that no crime had been committed and emphasized that Hugh continued to work

full time, attend group, and report to his probation officer as required. The prosecutor, relatively new, had difficulty putting forth a compelling reason why Hugh should be sanctioned for his less than stellar participation in group. The probation officer was able to detail why full participation in group was necessary and with documentation spell out what Hugh had agreed to in the treatment contract, and what efforts were made over time to assist Hugh in meeting his responsibilities. The documentation showed the number of opportunities Hugh was given to complete his homework and to address his failure to pay for treatment.

The judge was convinced that the probation officer and therapist appeared to be doing all the work and that Hugh had not lived up to his probation agreement. The judge revoked Hugh's probation, ordered a short jail sentence and a continuance of probation with enhanced conditions of probation.

The use of a paper chain to document not only the seriousness of the behavior, but what steps have previously been taken with offenders to control their risk forms the basis for proving the violation. When bringing a violation be sure to have the following documentation:

(1) Treatment agreement and case plan signed and dated by the offender
(2) Waiver of limited confidentiality form signed and dated by the offender
(3) Written warnings given to the offender regarding supervision or treatment signed and dated by the offender
(4) Documentation regarding offenders' acceptance of responsibility for their offense
(5) Documentation of progress or lack of progress made by the offender in addressing risk factors, developing coping strategies to deal with high-risk situations and follow through on the case plan
(6) Documentation of whether the offender has failed to report lapse behaviors, how lapse behaviors were discovered, and what the consequences were of discovering the unreported lapse behaviors

Testifying in Court

Testifying in court produces anxiety even for the seasoned professional. A forensic psychiatrist, who had testified at numerous hearings over a forty-year career, admitted that he always felt nervous before testifying. Instead of seeing this as negative, however, the psychiatrist viewed his anxiety as positive; he said his pretestifying anxiety resulted in his being well-prepared. And, for the probation officer, being prepared for court testimony is essential.

The probation officer usually is required to testify in court in two situations: at a sentencing hearing after completing a presentence report or at a violation hearing after the offender has violated conditions of probation. There also may be the occasion when the probation officer must testify at a trial. Regardless of the type of hearing, certain areas should be noted.

1. **Be prepared**—Be familiar with the documents that you have prepared, including the presentence report, case notes, or the violation paperwork. Be ready to defend your opinions and recommendations. Meet with the prosecutor before the hearing and review what the expectations are. Discuss questions that may be forthcoming by the defense attorney. Discuss with the prosecutor any anticipated problems. You do not want to surprise the prosecutor by giving unexpected information on the stand.

2. **Maintain the stance of an expert**—As a corrections professional, you should be an expert on risk control and risk reduction. Risk control is the supervision strategy designed to reduce the offender's opportunity to relapse, such as imposing a curfew or restricting the operation of a vehicle. Risk reduction is designed to address the offender's risk areas contributing to the sexually deviant behaviors, such as engaging in sex-offender treatment. Be prepared to answer questions regarding supervision issues, such as the necessary conditions of probation (and why), and the level and type of supervision that will be provided, such as electronic surveillance, polygraphs, intensive and/or team supervision.

Although you may be very knowledgeable about treatment issues, you are not a therapist. Avoid the trap of making a treatment assessment. The defense attorney may attempt to lead you in this direction and then discredit you. Be wary. Never forget this is an adversarial arena. However, you should be aware of sex-offender treatment resources in your community and be prepared to justify why a particular therapist is not used by your department. For example, if the offender wants to continue to see a therapist who, in your opinion, does not have the expertise, the judge may ask you for your rationale in denying that client's preference (see Questions for the Therapist, page 92).

3. **Dress conservatively**—In many offices, casual dress is not only allowed but encouraged because of the fieldwork involved. However, the courtroom is a formal and conservative setting. You will increase your credibility as an expert witness if your attire is appropriate for the setting.

4. **Maintain proper demeanor**—Maintain eye contact with the person who is asking the questions. Avoid facial expressions or gestures to make a point. The court reporter only can record what you say, not what you do. Be aware of posture. Avoid fidgeting with your hands. Be objective in your representation. You may not like the

defense attorney, but do not allow your body language to convey this. If you do, you are jeopardizing your credibility as an objective witness. Do not show anger or defensiveness. There is plenty of time off the stand to rehash the testimony with your colleagues and let down your guard.

5. **Use appropriate language**—Avoid jargon. Be aware of the shortcuts that are used in talking with other corrections professionals, but remember that part of the reason you are in court is to educate. You will not be educating if you use a vocabulary with which lay people are unfamiliar. Describe your job in everyday terms. Avoid use of superlatives such as "always" and "never." Avoid words such as "I think," "I guess," and "kind of" (Resnick, 1988). Although the courtroom is not always solemn, do not attempt to be humorous.

6. **Be prudent and judicious in answering questions**—Listen to the question. Pause before answering, if necessary. Give short, clear answers. Do not volunteer information. If you do not understand a question, ask for clarification or repetition. Do not answer a question that you do not fully understand. Do not guess. It is okay to say you do not know or that you do not remember. Avoid giving a yes or no response to questions that begin with "Wouldn't you agree that it's reasonable . . ." or "Isn't it possible . . ." (Resnick, 1988). A clear and specific response will avoid misleading or inaccurate information.

7. **Be careful of the defense attorney's summarizing for you**—Correct any error, however small, if the defense attorney summarizes a prior statement you made. If there were three factors that led to your recommendation of incarceration and the defense attorney names only two, you should correct this politely but firmly.

It is the role of the probation officer to be as clear and concise as possible in providing testimony. Do not take on the role of other designated court personnel when testifying. Remaining with your role, which is the supervision of the sex offender, is the best course.

Supervision Transfers

Transferring offender supervision to a different jurisdiction, whether within the state or out of state, requires planning to ensure the transfer is appropriate. The availability of specialized treatment in the receiving jurisdiction and the appropriateness of the proposed residence and employment must be considered, as well as whether the special conditions of probation or parole can be met.

The offender's offense and risk factors often dictate the amount of information and verification that must occur. In states where services and supervision vary from district to district, researching information for transfers in-state take on almost the same proportions as out-of-state transfers. The following are types of information that should be gathered before a transfer is considered.

(1) Look for sufficient safeguards in place for the offender to live safely in the community. Is a convicted child molester proposing to move to a housing complex which has a large proportion of single mothers and children?

(2) Ensure the offender will have some type of support in the receiving area. Family or friends of the offender must be knowledgeable about the offense and risk factors and believe the offender committed the offense. The individuals at the receiving site must be willing to interact with the probation/parole officers to ensure the offender is in compliance with imposed conditions and treatment. If the relatives/friends receiving the offender into their community have long-standing problems with authority, their reliability as reporters of high-risk behaviors on the part of the offender would be questionable.

(3) Ensure the offender is not proposing employment that presents risk to the community and potential victims. If an offender molested children from his church and was requesting transfer to a music teacher's position in a school setting, the job would be unacceptable. Such a request would also indicate the offender's level of denial around his deviant behaviors.

(4) Verify that specialized treatment services will be available for the sex offender.

(5) Ideally, the receiving probation/parole office should practice specialized supervision of sex offenders that recognizes the persistent and compulsive nature of sexually deviant behavior. Determine whether the receiving probation/parole office has received training in working with sex offenders.

Transfer of supervision also may include movement of an offender's case to another probation/parole officer within the same office. When this occurs, the new officer, after reading the file, should ask the offender to recount details of the offense, the risk factors, and relapse plan. The restating of this information reinforces to the offender the seriousness of the deviant behavior, the responsibility inherent in managing deviant behaviors and demonstrates to the new officer the level of responsibility the offender assumes in regard to deviant behaviors.

Travel Permits

Permission to travel is a privilege, not a right. Before granting permission for a sex offender to travel, planning must occur to ensure community safety as well as a method to monitor the offender's activities. In the early stages of supervision, travel may be denied routinely until the framework of supervision is established and the offender has engaged meaningfully in treatment.

Offenders request travel for a variety of reasons: business, family matters, and pleasure. Each request may carry a set of circumstances that requires planning on the part of the offender. For a travel request to be considered, a number of conditions must be satisfied:

(1) Offenders must be in compliance with the court-imposed conditions. Offenders who have failed to meet financial obligations, have pending charges, or missed meetings with the probation/parole officer or therapist should be denied their request, unless there are mitigating circumstances that have been evaluated by the probation/parole officer.

(2) Offenders have acknowledged full responsibility for the offenses for which they have been convicted, and have been forthcoming about risk factors.

(3) Offenders must be progressing in treatment and demonstrating the ability to impose controls over their deviant behavior.

(4) Offenders must be truthful in disclosing their offense and areas of risk to the supervision network as directed by the probation/parole officer.

(5) The request must not have an adverse affect on the community, the victim, potential victims, or the offenders' ability to control their risk to reoffend.

(6) Determine whether there were problems from previous travel requests.

(7) Ensure the request for travel does not interfere with the offender's treatment or employment.

(8) Offenders must be truthful in documenting reasons for the travel request. The request for travel must be made in advance.

This is not an exhaustive list, but it highlights some of the areas the probation/parole officer will want to explore. Differences in offenders and their risk factors will warrant varying levels of scrutiny in considering the travel request.

If a travel permit is to be granted, the following types of documentation should be present:

- The offender must fully complete the request for travel. This includes the means of travel, license number, flight numbers, time, and route. Indicate whether the offender is traveling alone or accompanied. Indicate if the offender's travel companion is aware of the offender's offense and risk areas. Verify that any travel companion is not an offender.

- Indicate who the offender is visiting and include names, addresses, and phone numbers of individuals at the residence. They should be aware of the offender's offense and risk areas. Note others who are likely to be visiting the residence. Indicate the relationship between the offender and individuals at the travel destination. Note any potential areas of risk at the offender's destinations. A phone call can retrieve some information if there is any doubt. Determine if the offender has visited the destination previously. If the travel request covers more than two weeks, monitor by calling the offender at the number the offender provided.

- Prepare the form letter that the offender is to present to the law enforcement agency in the area to which he traveled. The form letter (see page 130) must be signed by a law enforcement official and include a phone number for purposes of verification.
- In treatment, the offender should prepare risk scenarios that could occur on the trip. Rehearsing these situations with coping and escape strategies may help the offender anticipate and successfully deal with potential lapses.

Offenders with business obligations that require frequent travel outside the state may not be allowed to keep this type of employment; an example is that of the long distance truck driver. Travel should be easy to verify and monitor. If the offender is accompanied by someone, that person must be fully informed of the offender's risks and be willing to participate in the supervision network.

Vacation requests should be received well in advance. Last-minute vacation requests from offenders generally show lack of planning or a resistance to having their requests scrutinized. Offenders must initiate their own travel requests. Travel requests should not be made by the offenders' spouses or parents.

Some requests for travel are unforeseen, such as the death of a relative. This is often a time when sympathetic family members may relax the rules or let down their guard. The probation/parole officer may find him or herself in the same position. It is always better to be vigilant in such situations and as time and resources permit, perform the same type of research before granting the request that would be done under normal circumstances. It is important to diminish the opportunity for the offender to relapse.

The following are two common examples of requests for travel, both for legitimate reasons, both with different results.

Example A

Harvey was convicted of child molesting. He was a football coach at a university and required to travel annually out of state to recruit potential players. Although apparently progressing well in treatment and responsive to supervision, the probation officer had some reservation about granting the request. After researching the request with positive results, the probation officer granted the request. Harvey was given a travel permit along with a letter to law enforcement agencies indicating Harvey's status as a sex offender. The letter was to be presented to the police department in the receiving area and signed with a contact number by the officer in charge. Upon return from his trip,

Harvey presented the signed law enforcement letter to the probation officer. The probation officer called the police officer designated on the letter. The police officer denied ever meeting the offender. Although seemingly a minor offense, Harvey demonstrated that he still could not be trusted and had manipulated the system to meet his own needs.

Example B

Jim requested permission to travel out of state to visit his mother who was seriously ill. After ensuring that he would be accompanied by his wife who was fully aware of her husband's risk factors as well as details of his offense, permission to travel was granted. The probation officer required Jim to present the law enforcement letter to the area police department indicating his status as a convicted sex offender.

Jim showed up for his regular appointment with the probation officer and indicated he decided not to visit his mother after all. The change in plans made the probation officer suspicious, so he called the police department in the area that Jim was to visit. The officer in charge did a quick record check, and the probation officer learned that there was an outstanding warrant for child molestation from two years previous. Jim's presentation of the letter to law enforcement would have alerted authorities.

Although both requests were for legitimate reasons, there is good reason to research travel requests, and doing follow-up work can reveal a great deal of information. The information uncovered could reveal problems that require attention.

Chapter 4

Tools for Assessing Compliance and Control

Technologies exist today that have produced tools useful to the probation/ parole officer in assessing the offender's compliance and helping the offender control his deviant urges.

Penile Plethysmography

The penile plethysmograph is used to measure the erectile response in males. During this procedure the client is instructed, in the privacy of the laboratory room, to place a gauge onto the shaft of his penis. The gauge is connected to the chart recorder which is in the adjoining room, as is the evaluator who has verbal contact with the client during the evaluation. The client, seated in a recliner, is presented with both deviant and nondeviant sexual stimuli, and the gauge detects change in the size of the penis. The erectile response, which is recorded on a strip chart operated by the evaluator, provides a record of the client's arousal pattern. The stimuli typically used are audiotapes or slides.

When audiotapes are used, the client is given a set of earphones. The audiotapes include both normal and deviant sexual activity of both sexes. The typical scenarios include fondling, consenting/nonforceful intercourse, coercive sex, rape, and physical assault with both children and adults of both sexes (Association for the Treatment of Sexual Abusers 1993). When slides are used, the image is projected on the

Pithers and Laws (1988) indicate numerous advantages for the inclusion of the penile plethysmograph in a comprehensive treatment program as it provides for:

(1) identification of individuals who manifest excessive arousal in response to stimuli depicting sexual abuse
(2) discernment of lack of arousal to stimuli of consenting sex
(3) identification of offenders whose arousal disorder necessitates specialized behavioral therapies
(4) minimization of distortions evident in self-reported level of arousal
(5) evaluation of therapeutic efficacy
(6) enhancement of certain forms of behavioral therapy

wall or screen in front of the client. The typical slides include both nude and clothed poses of males and females of varying ages.

There has been controversy in recent years over the use of photographic slides, and in 1995, the Association for the Treatment of Sexual Abusers recommended that slides no longer be used. There were concerns about the lack of informed consent waivers on some of the photographs, and many practitioners felt the children in the photos were being revictimized. The recent development of computer-generated images of children will provide standardization and eliminate the need for releases. The Association for the Treatment of Sexual Abusers is supporting the use of computer-generated images.

Although the penile plethysmograph is a valuable assessment instrument for clinicians, it is not a lie detector nor is it a pass-fail test. It measures sexual arousal only. Moreover, a client's sexual arousal to a particular deviant stimuli does not mean he has acted on this arousal. Therefore, this instrument never should be used to argue a client's guilt or innocence to a particular charge. The penile plethysmograph is only one of many assessment tools used with sex offenders and should not be used independently of other assessment measurements (Association for the Treatment of Sexual Abusers 1993).

Though important in the evaluation and treatment process, the penile plethysmograph has its limits (Pithers and Laws 1988). One is the ability of some clients to inhibit their arousal to deviant stimuli. This may be more a problem in an incarcerated setting where offenders have the opportunity to exchange suppression strategies with one another. The competence of the evaluator in detecting suppression will be important in these situations. Another limitation is the failure of the laboratory setting to approximate the real world. For example, some rapists become more deviantly aroused when angry or under the influence of alcohol, and some offenders may be so anxious that arousal is curtailed in the laboratory setting. A final limitation is the lack of standardization in both testing and interpretation of the penile plethysmograph's finding. In response to lack of standardization, the Association for the Treatment of Sexual Abusers has developed guidelines for the use of the penile plethysmograph (1993). These guidelines can be obtained through the Association for the Treatment of Sexual Abusers, P.O. Box 866, Lake Oswego, Oregon 97034.

Polygraph

The polygraph often is referred to as a "lie detector test." In fact, the polygraph measures emotional arousal that is brought about by fear, not lying. The polygraph instrument measures physiological reactions associated with arousal of the autonomic nervous system such as increased heart activity, rate and depth of breathing, and palmar sweating (Lykken 1981, Reid and Inbau 1977). These reactions reflect fear, and it is this physiologic response that is interpreted by polygraph examiners as indicating truth or deception. Therefore, it is the fear of being caught in a lie that is being measured by the polygraph, not the lie itself.

The polygraph has been as controversial as the plethysmograph although for different reasons. The plethysmograph has passed the test on reliability and validity, but the invasiveness of the procedure has continued to be an issue with its critics. On the other hand, the polygraph has been criticized on the issue of reliability and validity. Despite the controversy, it has been used for many years by police, defense attorneys, the federal government, and private businesses. It is not uncommon for a district attorney's office to decide not to press charges if the defendant passes the polygraph test.

The use of the polygraph in court procedures in some states remains controversial and often is decided on a case-by-case basis. In recent years, it has been widely used by therapists and correctional departments in the treatment and supervision of sex offenders with acclaimed success. An Oregon law states that polygraph monitoring can be made a condition of probation (Oregon Revised Statutes 137,540 2-A) and Oregon courts have upheld this law (State v. Victoroff, 90 OR APP 171 [1989]).

Two basic polygraph techniques are used when working with sex offenders. The first is the discovery or disclosure test that is typically administered after an offender has been in treatment for three-to-six months. The second technique is the maintenance polygraph, administered on a routine basis to check on supervision and treatment compliance.

Prior to the disclosure test, sex offenders would work on completing their sexual autobiography in the initial stages of treatment. A polygraph would be administered after the completion of the sexual autobiography to verify the offenders' level of honesty with their sexual autobiography. From the beginning, offenders are told that they will be having a polygraph and knowing this in advance helps them develop a more complete sexual autobiography. Using this technique, offenders are asked questions about further disclosures before the polygraph, and if deception is detected during the polygraph, offenders are given the opportunity to discuss or clarify those issues. The purpose of the disclosure test is to obtain as complete a sexual history as possible so that treatment will address all needed areas of sexual deviance.

The maintenance polygraph usually is administered every six months. The focus with the maintenance polygraph is on supervision and treatment compliance. The administration of the periodic polygraph has a deterrent value (Abrams 1989, Abrams and Ogard 1986) as offenders may be more reluctant to engage in illegal or deceitful acts knowing that the polygraph will be administered on a regular basis. Although most programs using the polygraph will not use the failure of the polygraph test as the sole basis for a probation/parole violation, the failure can result in increased supervision by the probation/parole officer and/or confrontation in the offender's treatment group.

However, with the advantages also come disadvantages to the use of the polygraph. One disadvantage is if sex offenders have rationalized their behavior to the point that they do not regard it as problematic, they may not become anxious when asked a relevant question regarding sexual activity on the polygraph exam (Cross and Saxe 1992). Therefore, some sex offenders who have committed sexual offenses may "pass" the lie detector test. Some types of offenders also show an increased risk of error, such as the mentally disordered or the severely intoxicated (Raskin 1986). There is also the problem of the false positive polygraph test result. Saxe *et al.* (1985) showed that innocent subjects may face a higher risk of polygraph error than guilty subjects. The fact that disclosure and maintenance polygraph testing is used after the guilt of the sex offender has been established does reduce the problem of false positive results.

Polygraph Standards

- Inform your department's legal division and your district attorney/parole board of your plans. If they have concerns, you will want to address them prior to implementation of the program. They may have additional guidelines that they will want you to follow. Having them on board is essential even if your intention is not to use the polygraph as a basis of a violation.

- The qualifications of your polygraphers will be important to the integrity of your program. It is helpful from the start to standardize the disclosure and maintenance tests. If you are in an area where polygraphs are already used and there is no standardization, you may want to arrange a meeting of all your polygraphers and begin the process of standardization.

- Probation/parole officers need to be ever vigilant in their supervision. Just because an offender passes the maintenance polygraph is not a guarantee that the offender is not being deceitful. Decreased level of supervision should never be made purely on the basis of a passed polygraph. Equally so, if an offender is showing possible deceit, it is not a guarantee the offender has violated a condition of probation/parole. It certainly means that there should be further questioning from the polygrapher; the probation/parole officer and therapist will also need to investigate possible problems.

The use of the polygraph with sex offenders has shown very promising results and is another important tool to be used by probation/parole officers in their supervision practices. When a probation/parole department decides to use the polygraph in the supervision of sex offenders, it is important to set standards prior to application:

Psychopharmacology

Some sex offenders have repetitive and intrusive deviant sexual fantasies that occur so frequently as to interfere with their concentration. Other offenders have used behavioral techniques that have not reduced successfully their deviant arousal. Psychotropic medications such as antipsychotic medication, antiandrogens, and mood stabilizers have been prescribed over the years to help control this sexual activity.

The antiandrogen medroxyprogesterone acetate drug, more commonly known as Depo-Provera, has been used with some success with these offenders. However, Depo-Provera, sometimes referred to as chemical castration, is not the cure-all for which some people wish. This drug reduces the level of sexual arousal by acting upon the hypothalamus which stimulates the pituitary to release the hormones that control the production of sperm. Men using this drug can still obtain an erection, ejaculate, and engage in sexual intercourse. However, there are adverse side effects to this drug, and offenders with preexisting diabetes, obesity, or pulmonary disease are advised against taking it. Within a short time after stopping the drug, the androgen levels return to normal.

In recent years, antidepressant and antiobsessional drugs, such as Prozac and Anafranil, have been used to assist in the reduction of deviant fantasies and sexual impulses. Kafka (1994) reports selective serotonin reuptake inhibitors (SSRIs), especially fluoxetine (Prozac) and chlomipramine (Anafranil), to be helpful with men with paraphilia disorders. The theory is that obsessive-compulsive disorder and compulsive sexual behavior may both involve serotonin, therefore SSRI's which inhibit serotonin, could be beneficial for some sex offenders. Drug treatment should never be used unless the offender is involved in a treatment program and is under the supervision of a physician.

Chapter 5

Theories of Sexual Deviance

Many theories over the years have attempted to explain the causes of sexual deviance. Is it biological, cultural, or societal? A single theory has yet to explain fully the cause of sexual abusive behaviors.

As with many aberrant behaviors, several factors or a combination of factors could be causal in the development of sexually abusive behavior. The two models described below consider the various influences that impact on human behavior.

Finkelhor and Araji (1983) developed a multifactor model to explain child molestation. This model integrates a variety of single factor theories as an avenue to explain the causes of sexual deviancy.

The first factor, **emotional congruence**, looks at why an adult would experience sexual involvement with a child to be emotionally satisfying. Theories that take this approach look at child molesters as being immature, having low self-esteem, and having difficulties in their relationships with adults. It also takes into consideration child molesters who were sexually abused as children and may be using children sexually to overcome their own childhood trauma of powerlessness and shame.

The second factor, **sexual arousal**, looks at why an adult would find a child to be sexually arousing. Social learning theory looks at early sexual experiences, whether they are pleasurable, embarrassing, or shameful, as possibly conditioning the person to find children sexually arousing. Even a traumatic victimization in childhood may lead to the imprinting of the event in his or her sexual arousal.

The third factor, **blockage**, looks at why an adult would not obtain emotional and sexual needs from other adults. Blockage is divided into two categories. The developmental blockage, which is more chronic, refers to the failure to move through the normal developmental phases leading to adulthood. The situational blockage refers to a current crisis, such as a deteriorating marriage in the case of an incest offender, as the cause of seeking a sexual outlet through the children.

The fourth factor, **disinhibition**, looks at why societal norms and legal consequences do not prevent an adult from molesting children. Examples of disinhibitors are poor impulse control, senility, alcoholism, and psychosis. Situational stressors, such as unemployment or loss of relationship, also would be regarded as disinhibitors.

Schwartz and Cellini (1995) propose a model that includes both rapists and child molesters. In this model, there are two components to any criminal act: a motive and a releaser. For the sex offender, a motive may be sexual arousal, anger, lack of power, fear of women, distorted attitudes, or a combination of these. The releaser is what allows the sex offender to engage in the behavior despite personal or societal sanctions. Releasers include stress, lack of empathy, cognitive distortions, substance abuse, pornography, peer pressure, mental retardation, psychosis, and/or brain damage. Environmental controls and victim attributes also will factor into whether an assault actually occurs.

Dynamics of Sexual Assault

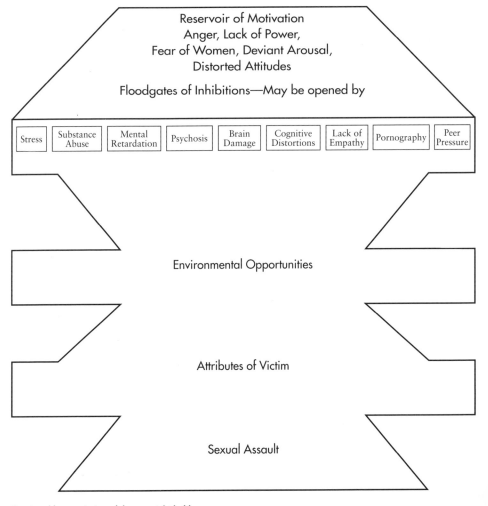

Reservoir of Motivation
Anger, Lack of Power,
Fear of Women, Deviant Arousal,
Distorted Attitudes

Floodgates of Inhibitions—May be opened by

| Stress | Substance Abuse | Mental Retardation | Psychosis | Brain Damage | Cognitive Distortions | Lack of Empathy | Pornography | Peer Pressure |

Environmental Opportunities

Attributes of Victim

Sexual Assault

These two models imply that the treatment of the sex offender requires a variety of treatment modalities. Reducing deviant sexual arousal may involve behavioral techniques to recondition sexual preferences or the use of medications, such as serotonin reuptake inhibitors (SRI's) or Depo-Provera, to reduce arousal. Lack of sexual knowledge, poor social skills, and difficulties with anger may involve psychoeducational treatment components. Instilling victim empathy could involve both psychoeducational components and role playing the offender's offense.

Typologies of Sex Offenders

Typology is the study of a class or group that has common characteristics. Sex-offender typologies can be helpful in distinguishing different groupings of offenders and predicting the types of future behavior in which offenders may engage, but it is equally important not to overlook individual differences or the possibility that a sex offender may engage in several different types of behavior. Two problems with typologies is the tendency to fit a particular offender into a category that may not fit or failure to acknowledge that an offender may exhibit behaviors from two or more categories in a typology.

The typologies outlined below were developed for law enforcement agents to assist in sexual assault investigations. These typologies were chosen because of their usefulness for probation and parole officers in anticipating what risks an offender may pose under supervision and/or what behaviors the offender may exhibit during the grooming phase toward a reoffense.

Child Molesters

Groth (1978) developed a classification that divided child molesters into two categories: the **fixated** child molesters who have a primary sexual attraction to children that has been constant throughout their life; and the **regressed** child molesters who have a primary sexual attraction to adults but due to situational stressors, such as unemployment or marital difficulties, resort to children for sexual gratification. Lanning (1986) developed a typology that used Groth's classification and adapted it for use by law enforcement agents. The two categories with their subtypes are as follows:

Situational Child Molesters   The sexual preference of this type of child molester is not solely children and he may resort to victimizing other vulnerable populations such as the disabled or the elderly. There are four basic patterns:

Regressed—This offender usually has low self-esteem and poor coping skills. They use children as a sexual substitute and their main criterion for choosing a victim may be availability. Stress, such as job loss or marital problems, may precipitate the sexual abuse. This type most closely resembles Groth's regressed child molester.

Morally Indiscriminate—This offender is criminally oriented, using and abusing people indiscriminately. He selects victims by opportunity and vulnerability. He may use force or manipulation to obtain victims, and although his victims are frequently strangers or acquaintances, he may also abuse his own children. This type of offender is particularly high risk to abuse pubescent children. His abuse of people is not always sexual.

Sexually Indiscriminate—This offender's basic motivation is sexual experimentation. He has no real sexual preference for children and appears to sexually victimize children out of bordeom. He may be involved in a variety of sexual activity, both criminal and non-criminal, such as multiple adult partners, prostituting his children and spouse swapping. His profile includes multiple victims and collecting pornography. He is more likely to be otherwise law abiding except in his sexual practices and often is from a higher socioeconomic background.

Inadequate—This offender is more of a social misfit who may become sexually involved with children out of curiosity or insecurity. The child victim may be a stranger or someone he knows. This offender finds children to be non-threating objects and the sexual activity with children is often a result of built-up impulses. Some of these offenders find it difficult to express anger and hostility. These offenders may also suffer from psychoses, senility and/or an intellectual disability.

Although any type of child molester may murder their victim, the FBI Behavioral Science Unit (Lanning 1986) has found the morally indiscriminate and inadequate to have murdered their victims more often then the other two subtypes in this category.

Preferential Child Molesters   The sexual preference of this type of child molester is solely children. They may have age and sex preferences and engage in predictable patterns of sexual behavior with their child victims. They are smaller in number than the Situational Child Molester but they have the potential to molest large numbers of victims.

Seduction—This offender engages in lengthy grooming of his victims, he knows how to talk to children and listen to them. This offender seduces children by gradually, over time, lowering their sexual inhibitions. This offender typically selects children who are emotionally or physically neglected. He may be molesting several victims during the same time period. The major difficulty for this type of offender is not how to obtain child victims but how to terminate when the victim gets too old. Victim disclosure may occur during this time and the offender may use threats or violence to avoid the secret being disclosed.

Introverted—This offender prefers children but lacks the social skills to seduce them. His victims typically are strangers or very young. He fits the old stereotype of the child molester who hangs around areas where children congregate such as school playgrounds or parks. This offender may also expose himself to children or make obscene phone calls. He may even marry a woman and have his own children. If this is the case, he is likely to sexually abuse them from the time they are infants.

Sadistic—This offender needs to inflict pain, psychological or physical, to become aroused. He is aroused by his victim's reponse to the infliction of pain or suffering. He may use force to gain access to his victim and is more likely than the other two subtypes to murder his victims. This type of offender is rare.

Rapists

Groth, Burgess, and Holmstrom (1977) also developed a typology for rapists. Their classification has four subtypes: the power-reassurance rapist, the power-assertive rapist, the anger-retaliatory rapist, and the anger-excitation rapist. Hazelwood (1995) expanded this typology and adapted it for use for law enforcement agents. Hazelwood's typology classifies rapists into six subtypes:

Power-reassurance—These rapists are unsure of their sexual adequacy and masculinity, and through forced sexual activity attempt to reassure themselves. They do not consciously intend to degrade or emotionally traumatize their victims. Typically, they do not use more force than necessary to gain submission and may apologize after the assault or attempt to recontact the victim. Their victims often are preselected through surveillance or Peeping Tom activities; the attacks generally occur at night. If the initial rape attempt is unsuccessful, they may strike again as quickly as the same evening.

Power-assertive—These rapists do not doubt their sexual adequacy or masculinity and use rape to express their dominance over women. These offenders usually do not resort to excessive force but have a detached and macho attitude.

They may assault the victim repeatedly and rip and tear the victim's clothing. If they have driven the victim to a secluded area, they often will leave the victim stranded, thereby delaying the victim's ability to report the crime.

Anger-retaliatory—These rapists have anger toward women in general and use sex as a weapon to degrade and punish. They use excessive force, and the initial attack will be of a physical nature so as to deny the victim any opportunity to defend herself. Often, there is no pattern to the rapes as they are triggered by anger and rage, and may occur during the day or at night. For the victim, the selection is often the result of being at the wrong place at the wrong time. The rape itself is often of short duration, with the offenders leaving when their pent-up anger has been vented.

Anger-excitement—These rapists derive pleasure from the suffering of their victims. The primary motivation is inflicting pain. The victim's response of fear and/or submission is what is sexually stimulating to these offenders. Although this type of rapist is rare, his attacks are vicious and result in serious physical and emotional trauma to the victim.

Opportunistic—This type of rapist may be committing another crime and rape a woman who is at the crime scene. The motivation is primarily sexual in nature. For example, if an offender is robbing a home, he may discover a woman is there alone or with young children. Hazelwood (1995) warns that it is important not to confuse this offender with a rapist who consistently rapes during the commission of other crimes.

Gang Rape—In rapes that involve two or more offenders, typically there is a leader in the group. At times, there is a reluctant participant when the gang consists of three or more participants. It is the reluctant participant who may be described by the victim as more protective or helpful. It is the reluctant participant who is the weak link. Hazelwood recommends applying this profiling to each individual rapist within the gang.

Typologies should be used cautiously to avoid misleading labeling, although they can be important in assisting in the supervision strategies of probation/parole officers. These typologies have separated the rapists and the child molesters; yet, some rapists and child molesters will assault both adults and children, as the next study shows.

Abel *et al.* (1987), looked at the cross-over behaviors of sex offenders. For this research study, they obtained detailed sexual histories on 411 sex offenders. The participants were not incarcerated, were assured confidentiality, and only volunteers were accepted. To assure confidentiality, the participants were asked to withhold the specifics of any sex crimes that would lead to identification. They were assigned a confidential identification number, and a certificate of confidentiality from the secretary of Health, Education, and Welfare (*Federal Register* 1975) was obtained. Nearly 50 percent of the subjects in this study had engaged in multiple deviant behaviors.

For instance, of the 89 rapists in the study:

50.6 percent were involved in child molestation
29.2 percent were exhibitionists
20.2 percent were voyeurs
12.4 percent were involved in frottage
11.2 percent were sadists

Of the 232 child molesters in the study:

29.7 percent were exposing themselves to children and to adults
16.8 percent were involved in rape
13.8 percent engaged in voyeurism
 8.6 percent engaged in frottage
 5.6 percent were sadists

When incest offenders were questioned regarding other deviant sexual behavior, Becker and Coleman (1988) found:

44 percent had molested unrelated female children
11 percent had molested unrelated male children
18 percent had raped
18 percent had committed exhibitionism
 9 percent had committed voyeurism
 5 percent had committed frottage
 4 percent had committed sadism

These studies have significant ramifications for probation and parole officers and their supervision practices. Although there are some sex offenders who engage in one type of deviant behavior, there are those who engage in multiple deviant behaviors. This information has an impact, in particular, on the supervision of incest offenders, as it cannot be assumed they are not a risk to unrelated children. Despite the crossover with some sex offenders into different types of offending behavior, typologies remain useful.

Does Treatment Work?

Despite the rather large number of recidivism studies completed on sex-offender populations over the years, there remains the ongoing question of whether sex-offender treatment works. There has been particular concern about the effectiveness of treatment since the Furby, Weinrott, and Blackshaw (1989) review of sex-offender recidivism studies.

Furby *et al.* (1989) reviewed fifty-five recidivism studies including both treated and untreated sex offenders. They concluded, "There is as yet no evidence that clinical treatment reduces rates of sex reoffenses in general and no appropriate data for assessing whether it may be differentially effective for different types of offenders." The article also pointed out that many of the studies they evaluated used techniques that would be considered obsolete in today's standards of sex-offender treatment and that "there is always the hope that more current treatment programs are more effective." Quinsey *et al.* (1993) had a similar conclusion as Furby *et al.* in their review of outcome studies of sex offenders and concluded that "the effectiveness of treatment in reducing sex offender recidivism has not yet been demonstrated."

In response to the Furby *et al.* (1989) article, Alexander (1993) analyzed sex offender outcomes from sixty-eight recidivism studies. Alexander not only looked at the recidivism rate of treated offenders (10.9 percent) versus untreated offenders (18.5 percent) but compared the recidivism rate among treated offenders prior to 1980 (12.8 percent) to offenders treated after 1980 (7.4 percent). Alexander made this comparison due to cognitive-behavioral and relapse prevention modalities becoming more widespread in the treatment of sex offenders after 1980.

Alexander also looked at treatment modalities and found offenders treated with a combination of behavioral and group therapy had a recidivism rate of 13.4 percent, while offenders treated using the relapse prevention model combined with behavioral and/or group treatment reoffended at a significantly lower rate of 5.9 percent.

Marshall and Pithers (1994) reviewed outcome studies from five treatment programs that were using cognitive-behavioral interventions. The results of the Marshall and Pithers (1994) review were as encouraging as Alexander's (1993) review: "Although the studies reported or reviewed in these articles vary in methodological sophistication, they converge on the conclusion that sex offenders who have engaged in specialized treatment reoffend at lower rates than do offenders who have not participated in treatment." However, Marshall and Pithers (1994) also caution that "specialized treatment appears to have a greater influence on child abusers than rapists."

Hall (1995) reviewed twelve outcome studies with sex offenders that had occurred since the Furby *et al.* (1989) review. Hall wanted to address three issues:

"(a) Have the outcome studies since the Furby *et al.* (1989) review demonstrated the effectiveness of treatment with sexual offenders? (b) Is sexual offender treatment more effective for any particular type of sexual offender? and (c) Is any particular type of treatment more effective than other types of treatment with sexual offenders?" Hall concluded that "the results of the present meta-analysis suggest the effect of treatment with sexual offenders is robust, albeit small, and that treatment is most effective with outpatient participants and when it consists of hormonal or cognitive-behavioral treatments."

Although it appears that the issue of whether treatment of sex offenders is effective continues to be debated among researchers, the supervision of sex offenders in the community for the probation and parole officers remains a reality. In future studies, it would be helpful to look not only at the effectiveness of treatment techniques but the relationship of treatment and supervision, and whether supervision by specially trained officers can have an impact on treatment gains of sex offenders.

A recent recidivism study in Vermont shows encouraging results. In 1983, the Vermont Department of Corrections began to contract with therapists to provide specialized sex-offender treatment. The modality used was a group format using cognitive-behavioral and relapse-prevention techniques. The sex offenders were all court mandated into treatment and required to pay for the costs of their own treatment on a sliding-fee scale. The Department of Corrections supplemented treatment costs. To be accepted into treatment, the offenders were required to sign a limited confidentiality waiver which allowed the therapists to communicate freely with the supervising probation/parole officer. The probation/parole officers used relapse prevention as the supervising strategy.

From 1983 through 1993, a total of 690 sex offenders participated or were currently participating in the outpatient treatment program. The overall recidivism rate for the 690 offenders was 7.8 percent (54). Of the fifty-four reoffenders, forty were involved in treatment at the time of their reoffense and fourteen were no longer in treatment at the time of their reoffense. The recidivism rate for the offenders successfully completing treatment was .05 percent (1).

Is Treatment Cost Effective?

In close pursuit on the issue of treatment effectiveness is the debate about whether treatment is cost effective. Recidivism rates are important in evaluating the cost effectiveness of treatment.

McGrath (1995) analyzed the cost effectiveness of out-patient treatment. He used Vermont salaries to estimate the average cost of one reoffense. The costs included pretrial investigation, court costs, incarceration, incarcerated treatment, parole supervision, and victim-related costs. The average cost of a reoffense came to

$138,828. McGrath then estimated the costs of outpatient treatment in Vermont. With offenders paying on an ability-to-pay basis and the Department of Corrections supplementing the difference, the cost to the Department of Corrections is, on average, $346 per offender per year. The total cost of treatment per offender, based on three years of weekly treatment, is $1,038.

Using a cost-benefit model, McGrath examined savings for 100 treated versus 100 untreated sex offenders. The conclusions were that when there is no difference in the recidivism rate between treated and untreated offenders, the cost to the state is the additional $103,800 of treatment funds ($1,038 x 100) that the Department of Corrections spends to supplement the treatment groups. The savings start if recidivism is reduced by as little as 1 percent when the offender engages in treatment.

If one were to look at the results of Alexander's (1993) analysis of outcome studies in which treated sex offenders reoffended at 10.9 percent versus the untreated sex offender reoffending at 18.5 percent, it quickly becomes apparent that there are major savings in providing treatment options for sex offenders.

Chapter 6

H...

was tha...
the clie...
ual dev...

H...
recogni...
ment m...
with the ...
of treatment providers w...
cognitive-behavioral and relapse preventio...

However, within this format there is a multitude oi ...
used such as psychoeducational modules, behavioral treatment, family therapy, psychopharmacological options. A responsible treatment plan for a sex offender would identify the behaviors that predispose him or her to engage in sexually abusive behavior and then develop the appropriate treatment methods to correct the abusive behaviors.

Goals of Treatment

The Vermont Network of Sex Offender Therapists (1995), established in 1984, has recently completed a practice guideline for the assessment and treatment of sex offenders. Listed below is a brief summary of the six goals for treatment from the guidelines:

Accepting Responsibility and Modifying Cognitive Distortions

Treatment will confront denial, rationalizations, and cognitive distortions as well as educate offenders regarding the link between cognitive distortions and sexually aggressive behavior. Treatment will continue to evaluate the offenders' ability and

behavior, and accepting full
…eatment.

…h lectures, readings, audio-visual aids, and
…on victims. Treatment will assess the level and
…ers' ability to recognize and express emotional
…ropriate empathy.

…ousal

…e interventions to assist offenders in their ability to control,
…e deviant sexual arousal as well as assist offenders in the develop-
…, and strengthening of their appropriate sexual arousal. Assessment
…port, collateral information, psychological and plethysmograph testing.

…ving Social Competence

…eatment will address those social deficits that relate to the offenders' relapse pat-
…erns. Treatment will assess the offenders' ability to effectively deal with a variety of
situations that previously may have been precursors to reoffending.

Developing Relapse Prevention Skills

Treatment will identify offenders' relapse patterns and assist offenders in identifying
and interrupting their deviant sexual patterns. Treatment will assess offenders' ability to report precursors to sexually deviant behavior, as well as assess the appropriateness and success of their coping strategies.

Establishing Supervision Conditions and Networks

The therapist will assist the probation or parole officer in identifying both high-risk
factors and a collateral network of individuals to aid in the treatment and supervision of sex offenders.

Questions for the Therapist

In referring an offender to a sex-offender therapist, the probation/parole officer i
advised to inquire about the following:

1. Ask about the level of experience and training.

   The type of clinical degree is not as important as the experience and training. The therapist should have attended workshops on the issue of sexual deviancy and be familiar with both offender and victim issues. The field is established, and it is no longer necessary to learn by trial and error. However, new techniques and current research are acquired primarily through seminars or professional journals; therefore, it is important to ask if the therapist is continuing to update his or her skills.

2. Focus on offenders' deviant behaviors.

   The therapist should focus on the goals of treatment outlined at the beginning of this chapter. The therapist will need to be confrontative and direct in addressing deviant behaviors or patterns, yet within this framework remain respectful and nonpunitive toward offenders.

3. The therapist must work closely with the probation/parole officer.

   Therapists must require offenders to sign a limited waiver of confidentiality to allow for open communication with the probation/parole officer before accepting offenders into treatment (see page 131). If a therapist is not willing to do this, find another therapist. The working relationship with the therapist is a key ingredient to effective supervision, and a therapist who wants to work in isolation or will not talk to a probation/parole officer for fear of damaging the therapeutic relationship is promoting and encouraging the secret life of the sex offender. It is the inexperienced therapist who does not view the information received from a probation/parole officer as a valuable tool in the treatment process. Ensure that the therapist understands the importance of immediately notifying the probation/parole officer if dangerous or crisis situations occur.

4. The therapist must willingly testify in court.

   Not many people relish the idea of testifying in court. However, treating sex offenders will result in court hearings, and therapists going into this work need to understand and accept this as a reality.

5. The therapist must work as part of a team.

   Intrafamilial offenders and those sex offenders with psychiatric disorders and intellectual disabilities often require collaboration with other therapists and state agencies addressing mental health issues. Is the therapist a willing or reluctant partner in the team approach? The reluctant partner in the team may agree to participate, but when it comes to team meetings, he or she may take a passive role and rarely contribute information. It is critical that the therapist place community safety first while remaining within the ethical guidelines of the profession. Part of maintaining an ethical relationship with the sex offender is informed consent. The addendum has a sample of a confidentiality waiver and a treatment agreement, which provide the offender with informed consent before entering treatment.

6. The therapist should use a group format.

It is sex offenders' denial, manipulativeness, and secrecy that make them so difficult to treat individually. Barbara Schwartz (1988) says, "Group members are able to recognize their own patterns and may provide confrontation and support far more effectively than could the individual therapist." Group treatment is also more cost effective, which is a concern for probation/parole officers who more often have clients who cannot afford the individual therapy fee.

7. Assess the therapist's attitude toward sex offenders in denial.

Most sex offenders are in some form of denial when entering treatment; the issue is how much denial, and when is denial unacceptable for an offender in community supervision. A probation/parole officer's nightmare is the therapist who will accept anyone into treatment regardless of level of denial, and keep offenders in treatment for months with no breakthrough of the denial. This places the probation/parole officer in the position of supervising offenders who present high risk in the community and are making no changes to reduce their risk.

8. The therapist must work with offenders mandated into treatment.

Salter (1988) states the mental health community has traditionally opposed court-mandated treatment. However, sex offenders volunteering for treatment often do so to portray themselves in the best possible light to demonstrate a commitment to change during the legal process, and/or to return to their families. Once the pressure is off or when offenders have fulfilled their own needs, commitment to treatment generally wanes, and it is a matter of time before they stop attending. Therefore, mandated treatment is necessary to ensure that sex offenders remain in treatment until completion.

Probation/parole officers initially may feel uncomfortable in the role of questioning the qualifications of a therapist. However, the working relationship between the therapist and probation/parole officer is of paramount importance in the treatment and supervision of the sex offender, as are the skills of the therapist. A probation/parole officer is responsible for community safety and therefore will need to refer the sex offenders on his or her caseload to a therapist who will actively address the issues that contribute to the offender's deviant behavior and be in regular communication with the probation/parole officer.

Developing Treatment Resources

Many jurisdictions may not have ready access to therapists who are skilled or have experience working with sex offenders. Other jurisdictions may need to add to their existing clinical resources. In either case, the managers of a probation or parole office are faced with the task of finding clinicians to provide this essential service, and it will be necessary to develop a list of appropriate treatment resources for their officers to use when referring sex offenders for treatment. A periodic review of community resources is recommended to ensure availability of skilled, experienced therapists.

Resources may be close at hand and require only making contact with existing therapists who are known to have good reputations and demonstrated skill in working with offender populations. Other clinicians already may be seeing sex offenders in their practices and would welcome developing their skills to work more effectively with this population. Therapists already experienced in the work may know of colleagues who would be interested.

Letters to mental health agencies and private clinicians eliciting interest in working with this population can be sent out to gauge what the level of interest is in the community as well as what the skill level is of potential therapists. Advertise in the local papers. If the interest is there but not the skill, then the correctional department could sponsor specialized training for clinicians.

Another valuable resource for potential therapists is local colleges or universities. Schools with counseling programs are a valuable resource in the development of a network of therapists. Working with your experienced clinicians to provide internships for students is an avenue to increasing the number of clinicians in your area willing to work with sex offenders.

Interestingly enough, some jurisdictions have found that within their own ranks they have staff who have appropriate qualifications to work with this population. This often means restructuring the individual's job so it does not conflict with ethical guidelines and to avoid dual role relationships. However, it is not unusual to find probation and parole officers who have backgrounds in social work, mental health treatment, or counseling and psychology.

Correctional training related to supervising sex offenders should be offered to therapists to enhance the collaborative relationship between treatment and supervision. As therapists and correctional agencies work together, conflicts may arise regarding philosophy and practices between the two entities. Guidelines around roles and responsibilities of each must be developed to reduce inevitable conflicts. The focus of the work must remain on the sex offender. Working with sexually deviant offenders is demanding and often stressful. Supportive, collaborative relationships between therapists and corrections staff is the hallmark of the relapse prevention model.

Chapter 7

Reunification: Incest Families

W hen families wish to reunite, the process must be carefully and firmly supervised so that above all, the victim's healing, future growth, and well-being are not compromised. The probation/parole officer is pivotal in this process. When a knowledgeable probation/parole officer is aided by a skilled, experienced therapist, reunification may be achieved without ongoing or indeed, greater trauma to the victim, the nonoffending partner, or other children.

The probation officer's first contact with an incest offender usually occurs months after the abuse has been substantiated. Sometimes, coordinated protocols between police, social services, and the prosecutor have resulted in protection of the victim and siblings, support services for the nonoffending spouse, and a treatment referral for the offender. However, the probation officer may encounter an incest family in disarray. If this is the case, the presentence report becomes a vital tool in case planning. It is imperative that detailed conditions be set down in the presentence report that will closely direct and monitor the offender's behavior during the reunification process, if reunification is the goal of the family.

A vital condition is that in the initial stages of reunification, the offender live separately from the family, with the victim remaining in the home, if possible. It is also important to limit the offender's access to all minor children until there has been a psychosexual evaluation. Becker and Coleman (1988) found 44 percent of incest offenders in their study had molested nonrelated female children, and 11 percent had molested nonrelated male children. The restrictions on a probation warrant, of course, can be lessened over time when a more complete history of the offender has been obtained and the ability to engage appropriately in treatment has been shown.

The initial, total separation of the offender may be difficult for the family planning to reunite, especially if the offender has been living in the family home during the court proceedings. It is preferred that the victim remain in the family home, although it may not be possible in some circumstances. Giarretto *et al.* (1978) state exceptions should be made in the following situations: (1) the mother does not want the child to remain in the home, (2) the mother appears to be dangerously abusive, (3) the son/daughter is so beaten down and passive that he or she really cannot make this decision for himself or herself, and (4) the father's level of impulse control is extremely low, and he will have access to the family.

This separation of offenders from victims and family is key, not only for the protection of the victims, but also for spouses who will be undergoing their own conflicts. A group for spouses/partners of sex offenders can be of immeasurable benefit. Mothers may feel torn between loyalty toward their daughters or sons and their husbands or partners. In fact, they may feel conflicted about reuniting the family at all or may question if the abuse even has occurred. The most tragic outcome is when the offender has created an atmosphere of distrust and alienation between daughter or son and mother, making the rebuilding of the relationship between them problematic at a time when the victim most needs the love and support of her or his mother. Amid her own conflicts, the mother may feel isolated. A support group providing contact with other mothers who are struggling with similar issues can have a powerful and positive effect.

Meanwhile, the offender's progress in treatment will be one of the determining factors about when and if reunification of the family is to take place. The offender's readiness is crucial and entails more than the acceptance of responsibility for the sexually deviant behavior. Stermac *et al.* (1995) report that a large percentage (55 percent) of incest offenders demonstrated nonsexual forms of violence and abuse within their homes. This study indicates that incest offenders may have additional serious problems within the family unit beyond the sexual offense itself. Issues of power, control, and aggression beyond the incestuous behavior need to be addressed in the offender's treatment.

Other determining factors are both the victim's and the family's readiness. Many professionals working in the field have experienced decisions being made at the time of sentencing in which a judge has allowed a sex offender to return home with the victim, based purely on the offender's admission of guilt and apology in open court. This is inadequate. Marshall and Barbaree (1988) report that among sex offenders who remain untreated, there appears to be no difference in reoffense rates between deniers and admitters.

There are two essential conditions that must be met by the sex offender before reunification can begin. One is attitudinal in nature; the other requires mastery of skills (O'Connell *et al.* 1990). Incest offenders must take responsibility for their offense and move beyond denial, deceit, excuses, and justifications. They must understand how their behavior has harmed not only the victim but the family, and that their manipulation and abuse of power and control has jeopardized each individual's well-being and that of the family unit. Offenders must demonstrate empathy.

Aside from these attitudinal considerations, offenders must exhibit their ability to manage their arousal to deviant sexual stimuli. Concurrent with this, they must learn and use their relapse-prevention skills.

Therapists need the input from the probation officer and the social worker to complete their ongoing evaluation of how the family is doing outside the walls of their offices. The therapists must keep the probation officer and social worker informed of trouble spots and emerging risk factors that need to be monitored.

The first step in reestablishing contact is usually in the form of a letter written by the offender to his or her victim. Hindman (1990) refers to this as a clarification letter. Hindman emphasizes that a clarification letter is not an apology, rather the offender explains his or her manipulative behavior with no attempt to ask for forgiveness. This letter begins the process of clarifying and resolving for the victim what happened, and rewards the victim for disclosing the abuse. This is a letter that likely will require several drafts. The offender may ask the probation officer for advice or comment on progress with the letter, but the probation officer should be careful to avoid giving the offender direction in this assignment. At team meetings, the probation officer can discuss with the therapists the offender's request for help and the various responses possible that would assist the offender but not impede the therapeutic process that this exercise offers.

If the victim and family decide to move forward with the reunification process, a series of meetings between the victim, offender, and nonoffending spouse begin to occur. These meetings are facilitated by the victim and offender therapists. This is a slow process from the initial meeting between victim and offender to the offender moving back into the family home. Team meetings between therapists, probation officers, and social workers are important during this time in evaluating progress. Most therapists have a set of rules that establish the framework for reunification and clearly spell out the responsibilities of the offender and the nonoffending spouse. The probation officer and the surveillance officers need copies of these rules to enhance the effectiveness of their supervision.

One purpose of gradual reintegration is to identify small problems and work through solutions rather than risk unforeseen problems and further harm to family members. However, there is always the possibility that the reunification will fail, or that the victim may request a different time frame. The trust between the victim and his or her therapist will be essential in these instances.

Dwyer *et al.* (1992) assessed the behavioral effects of sex-offender treatment by interviewing seventy sex offenders post-treatment at intervals of six months, one, two, three, and four years. The feedback from the incest offenders in their sample is particularly revealing: "The least troubled participants were pedophiles, non-exclusive type, while the most troubled were former incest perpetrators. Often, however, the ex-incest offender did not seem to recognize the amount of family problems he still faced." The critical time for the participants in this study was at year three.

Successful reunification means the abuse stops and the family unit becomes a safe environment in which all the children become stronger and more assertive.

However, not all attempted reunifications succeed. Indeed, incest is so destabilizing and destructive to the qualities that permit family functioning, such as trust and refuge, that families may choose separation during the process.

For example, one incest family had been involved in a lengthy process of reunification with the father back in the home when the victim reported inappropriate behavior by the father (he was walking slowly by her bedroom at night after his wife had gone to bed). It was the mother who decided that the father was to leave the home and the reunification would stop. The victim immediately felt supported by her mother, unlike what had occurred during the initial disclosure in which the mother had been very ambivalent toward the victim and doubted the victim's account of the abuse.

There is very little written on the impact of culture on incest (Fontes 1995) and even less on how to work with families from diverse cultural backgrounds. Cultural misunderstandings can hinder the reunification process and cause further stress and chaos for the victim and family members. Cultural and religious beliefs must be taken into consideration by the team involved in reuniting incest perpetrators with their family. For further information, see "Ethnic and Minority Cultural Groups" in Chapter 9.

In summary, the probation officer is part of a team in the reunification of an incest family. Although many decisions will be made as a team, some of the enforcement will be clearly the responsibility of the probation officer. It is entirely appropriate for the probation officer to request the qualifications of the therapists involved in the reunification and to review their written protocol.

Chapter 8

Special Populations

S upervision and treatment of special populations present challenges that may appear overwhelming to probation and parole officers. The models and techniques outlined in this book can be modified successfully to apply in working with these populations.

Intellectually Disabled

In the early years of specialized sex-offender treatment, it was not uncommon for therapists to view intellectually disabled sex offenders as untreatable, or at the least, an extremely difficult population with an overall poor prognosis. Some professionals within the intellectually disabled field rationalized the sexual abuse and believed that the disabled offender should not be held accountable for the behavior. Sgroi (1989) points out that many professions still tend to infantilize the intellectually disabled adult when it comes to sexuality.

> The wishful expectation that physically normal adults with intellectual disabilities will not have or act upon sexual feelings or desires can be a covert barrier to recognizing sexual offense behavior when it does occur.

Although intellectually disabled sex offenders have special needs, they are by no means untreatable. In fact, there are many similarities between the nondisabled sex offender and the disabled sex offender. Both populations express levels of denial, lack empathy, and exhibit poor impulse control. Despite the similarities, there are still important differences to recognize and upon which probation and parole officers should act.

Haaven *et al.* (1990) point out three significant differences in their institutional treatment of the intellectually disabled sex offender. Although they were addressing treatment from an institutional perspective, the differences are pertinent to community supervision.

- A confrontational approach to denial was not effective. It was recommended denial be reduced by using an incremental disclosure approach, supported by arousal assessment data and staff tutors (for probationers/parolees, trained volunteers would be helpful).

- Intellectually disabled offenders had greater difficulty taking care of themselves and solving life crises, and as a result, they became more dependent on the program and staff.
- Self-esteem was particularly difficult to address because disabled offenders had fewer areas of competency. To compensate for these deficiencies, disabled offenders often exaggerated their accomplishments, were sensitive to criticism, overreacted to feedback, and were also more fearful of change.

Many therapists involved with this population prefer to have them in a separate sex offender group. This is often due to the amount of repetition needed to work with this population, the exposure of the offender to ridicule from other group members, and the slower pace of treatment due to the skill-deficiency level. However, the cognitive-behavioral and relapse-prevention approach is still applicable, as is group treatment. The use of additional support services, such as volunteers trained in working with sex offenders, is recommended. It is further recommended that volunteers commit to a long-term relationship as often intellectually disabled offenders must develop a positive working relationship with the volunteer before they feel safe enough to begin to address issues of sexual deviance.

Probation/parole officers must remain sensitive to the disabled offender's limitations. Educating the offender in the relapse prevention model will need to be accomplished using simple language and identifying a lower number of risk factors and coping strategies so as not to have too many new tasks for the offender to learn. It is important to be concrete. Intellectually disabled offenders often have difficulty generalizing one set of circumstances to other situations.

> Martin, thirty-one, spoke with his probation officer about being in the grocery store after work when a number of kids came into the store and headed to the same aisle Martin was in. The officer worked out with Martin that he would not go to the store immediately after work as that is the time kids are leaving school and going to the store on the way home. He further advised Martin that it would have been a good idea to leave the store when they came in and go straight home as he was to have no contact with minors.
>
> A week later Martin told the probation officer that he was at the bus stop waiting to go home from work when some kids appeared. He stated he was trying to get home and was scared. The officer reminded Martin he was not to be around minors and congratulated him for knowing that it was risky situation. The probation officer asked Martin if there was a safer way for him to get home. Martin said he knew of another bus stop that other people from work used. It was further but he could walk with them. It did mean he would have to leave work a little earlier, but he just would have to pick up his things and not stay

around and talk with co-workers after his shift. The probation officer gave Martin positive feedback on this new plan.

These examples show the need for specificity with these offenders as well as repetition. There will be many more situations that Martin will bring to the probation officer and his treatment group for assistance, especially if his disclosures are met with a nonjudgmental attitude and concrete ways for Martin to handle a potentially risky situation. Understanding these limitations will assist the offender in addressing high-risk situations.

Other areas to be aware of in working with this population is their need to please others and to not always be truthful rather than face disapproval. Although sex offenders must be challenged and confronted in the face of high-risk behaviors, the intellectually disabled offender may take a disproportionate amount of time to make changes in this area. It may require not challenging each and every piece of questionable information and not showing harsh disapproval when an offender shares information regarding some negative behavior. This is not to say risk should be overlooked or downplayed. How the officer or therapist addresses this behavior will go a long way in encouraging the offender to continue to share this information and learn other ways to behave.

Each individual in the offender's supervision network should be educated in the relapse-prevention approach and be willing to hold the offender accountable. They should also learn about issues regarding interactions with the intellectually disabled offender. It is a disservice to disabled offenders and their potential victims to view them as not capable of change.

Sgroi (1989) notes that in situations when two intellectually disabled adults are involved in a complaint as victim and perpetrator, there are a number of questions to be asked:

(1) Was the behavior consensual or was there resistance from the victim? Did the alleged victim protest or attempt to avoid the perpetrator?

(2) Do both individuals understand basic elements of sexual behavior? Do they understand elements of privacy, the right to exercise choice of a partner and the right of refusal? Even a lower functioning individual generally can distinguish between consequences for rubbing ears and rubbing genitals. Is there a past history on the part of the perpetrator to understand what "no" means as well as a past history of appropriately choosing a partner?

(3) Is there a power imbalance between the two individuals that precludes consent?

The evaluation and treatment of the intellectually disabled sex offender relies upon the recognition that the behavior is both sexual and abusive. Sgroi (1989) emphasizes that it is critical to become familiar with your state's sexual abuse statutes as well as policies regarding those deemed intellectually disabled to adequately meet the needs of this underserved population.

Psychiatric Disorders

Psychiatric disorders among sex offenders appear to be at the same rate as for the general population. Knopp (1984) suggests 5 to 8 percent of sex offenders have psychotic illnesses. If mental illness has been confirmed or is suspected, it may be helpful to have a psychiatric evaluation to assist in treatment planning. It may be that the client already is part of the mental health system. If so, a full psychiatric evaluation may not be necessary.

If a mentally ill sex offender is placed on probation, the coordination between mental health, sex-offender therapist, and probation officer will be essential. If the offender is under the care of a psychiatrist for psychotropic medication, the psychiatrist should be part of the multidisciplinary team. When the offender is being seen through a mental health agency with an on-site psychiatrist, the coordination of services may be easier.

The sex-offender treatment and mental health treatment fields do have different clinical approaches. It will be important that each become familiar with the treatment modalities, philosophy, and language of the other's discipline. Although there are differences, they are not incompatible. Confidentiality may be an initial stumbling block and will need to be addressed immediately. The monitoring of the offender's medication will be an important factor in the ongoing review of the offender's risk in the community, and the probation officer must have access to this information to provide the appropriate level of supervision.

Elderly

By the year 2010, individuals fifty and over will comprise 33 percent of the U.S. population (Moritsugu l990). According to the National Institute of Corrections (1986), 70 percent of older offenders are serving incarcerative sentences for violent offenses as compared to 56 percent of the younger offenders. Older incarcerated offenders are often believed to be quieter than other offenders; they present fewer security issues; they are less motivated to participate in correctional programs; and they experience an increased rate of health problems.

In working with the older sex offender on probation or parole, it is important to be knowledgeable about the normal aging process, such as physiological changes, diminishing but still present sex drive, and an increasing onset of mental health problems such as depression and dementia. The person who sexually abuses after the onset of senility presents special problems. Basic personality changes can occur with organic deterioration brought on by hardening of the arteries. This can effect the ability to control impulses such as anger and sexuality. Treatment is rarely a viable alternative for this type of offender, and supervision of the living environment will be imperative (Schwartz and Cellini 1995).

Chapter 9

Gender, Culture, and Youth

Any probation/parole officer working with a female or juvenile sex offender, or with a member of an ethnic or cultural minority group, should research typical concerns, behaviors, and customs for that population in order to supervise the client effectively. This chapter merely introduces a few possible areas of difference to take into consideration.

Female Sex Offenders

The traditional view of women is that they are nurturers, not criminals, and the women who do commit crimes are seen as atypical. This is a belief widely held with regard to the female sex offender who, like other female offenders, has been an anomaly in the criminal justice system.

Allen (1991) outlines three possible barriers to recognizing the child sexual abuse by women. The first barrier is the overestimation of the strength of the incest taboo. For many years, the incest taboo itself was enough to discount sexual abuse within the family unit, and the idea that the mother, the nurturer, may be the perpetrator was unthinkable.

The second barrier is the overextension of feminist explanations of child sexual abuse. The feminist theory sees child sexual abuse as a culturally based socialization process. In this theory, the male is dominant and sexually aggressive, while the woman is socialized to be the recipient of sexual encounters. Taking this theory to the extreme, women are socialized to be victims, not perpetrators; and, therefore, they are not perpetrators.

The third barrier is the overgeneralization of the lack of reports of child sexual abuse by women. Under this premise, the low frequency of reports leads to a common misinterpretation: few reports mean a low number of instances. Of course, all the literature on male sex offenders emphasizes that the reported incidence of sexual abuse is underreported. So, if that is true, why is it not equally true that sex abuse by females is underreported?

Allen (1991) emphasizes that recognizing these barriers is not to insinuate that the female rates of child sexual abuse may be equal to male rates; however, adherence to one or more of these beliefs could lead to underestimating the occurrence of female perpetrated sexual abuse. If the treatment needs of female sexual abusers are to be addressed adequately, their being abusers must be viewed as a problem, not an aberration.

Schwartz and Cellini (1995) reported that "research is contradictory whether one is studying gender differences in aggression, empathy, dependency, emotionality, sexuality, or cognition." Although the research is inconclusive on general gender differences, there do appear to be some basic differences between men and women who sexually abuse. The first is that a significant number of women appear to abuse with a male co-defendant. The second difference is that females are less violent than men during the offending behavior (Krug 1989). Third, the developmental issues for males and females are different, and treatment may need to be tailored to meet this difference.

A preliminary typology of female sex offenders was developed by Mathews (1987). Her groupings are teacher/lover, predisposed, and male-coerced.

The **teacher/lover** offenders typically abuse prepubescent and adolescent males, relating to the victim as a peer and lover. These women usually have a history of abusive relationships with adult males, and as a result have withdrawn from them.

The **predisposed** offenders typically abuse their own children and initiate the sexual abuse alone. They themselves are often victims of severe sexual abuse beginning at an early age. The motivation for these women is to achieve non-threatening emotional intimacy.

The **male-coerced** offenders act in conjunction with a male; the victims are children both within and outside the family. These women are extremely dependent, nonassertive, and endorse traditional roles for women. Sometimes the male-coerced offender will progress to initiating the sexual abuse, at times without her male co-defendant.

Although the treatment goals for female sex offenders remain the same as for males, Schwartz and Cellini (1995) report that the therapeutic philosophy in some of the treatment programs for females do differ:

> We do not know how much of these attitudinal differences are based on gender stereotypes. One may stress cognitive-behavioral therapy with males because it is assumed they are more cognitively oriented. Females may be nurtured or parented because it is assumed they are more emotional or dependent. Conversely, one may skirt the use of nurturance in treating males because one does not believe that males

respond to caretaking. Confrontation may be used with males because it is assumed that they are tough enough to handle it. Perhaps the central question concerns how much of the treatment of males is determined by the belief that they are bad and how much of the treatment of females is determined by the belief that they are mad. These issues can only be clarified by systematic research into the various treatment techniques and therapeutic assumptions.

For the probation/parole officer, however, the supervision issues remain very much the same as with male sex offenders. Supervision needs to focus on community safety with all the special conditions used for the male sex offender. Treatment remains essential, and the therapist must have expertise in treating sex offenders. Having a female abuser treated by a therapist who concentrates on the offender's victimization issues to the exclusion of her issues as an abuser or who views the sexual abuse as an aberration is counterproductive.

Not addressing sexual deviance perpetrated by females ignores the trauma caused by this behavior. However, this is still an issue fraught with emotion and controversy. Societal denial may remain one of the largest obstacles in working with this population. Denial around an issue that is perceived as shameful and repugnant, particularly when it involves women, is difficult to break through.

Ethnic and Cultural Minority Groups

The traditional view is that American culture is a fusion of various races and ethnic groups (the "melting pot"). From a blending of the many we achieve a commonality as Americans. Yet, the notion that we are a homogenous American culture, sharing the same values, beliefs, mores, customs, goals, and dreams is untrue. Even in the same culture there will be differences as a result of immigration/refugee experiences, acculturation levels, and socioeconomic levels (Philips 1996). Furthermore, many today celebrate cultural diversity, thwarting pressures to submerge their unique identities into that of the "melting pot." Some of today's immigrants, as well as existing minority populations, are not seeking admission to mainstream culture at all, but seek to keep their cultural identities intact, and to some degree, apart.

Behaviors are not only the result of the impact of culture but also may result from oppression (Fontes 1995). For example, the negative encounters that many African-Americans have had with the police and social service agencies may result in obstructing or delaying the reporting of child sexual abuse (Abney *et al.,* 1995). Colonialism, a policy that maintains foreign territories under the political jurisdiction of a dominant country, can be another form of oppression and can result in feelings of alienation, frustration, and poor self-esteem among the colonized people (Comas-Diaz 1995).

In discussing Puerto Ricans and sexual abuse, Comas-Diaz (1995) says:

> Sexual oppression and victimization may have been internalized as an aspect of colonization and simultaneously as an identification with its negative effects. In other words, sexual abuse may represent a familiar behavior with the polarities of power and powerlessness, and domination and subjugation.

Oppression, of course, affects both victim and victimizer and must not be ignored as a factor in the rehabilitation process.

The current literature on sexual abuse rarely addresses the impact of ethnic culture and oppression in the occurrence and treatment of sexual abuse (Fontes 1995). Separating the issues of culture and oppression in treatment may not be possible as long-term oppression does over time impact on culture. Despite the wide diversity of North American Jews, they remain vulnerable to anti-Semitism and widespread myths and stereotypes. Featherman (1995) says, "Searching for the meaning of sexual abuse in a certain family or for a certain individual involves a complex process that may be likened to an archaeological dig, where fragile fragments must be unearthed with patience and delicacy."

It is important, therefore, that individuals working with sex offenders first be aware of and sensitive to the diverse ethnic and cultural groups within their communities. Second, they must be aware of and be sensitive to the differences between similar ethnic groups. Third, they must be aware of what impact oppression may have on sexual abuse. Multicultural diversity training can help probation/parole officers become more responsive to the particular norms and beliefs of their clients, particularly when some sex offender techniques or strategies may run counter to certain ethnic groups' norms.

For example, the women's rights movement of the 1960s and 1970s in the United States had a major and positive impact on how we, as a society in America, responded to sexual abuse, but our cultural shift regarding the status of women and children was not necessarily adopted by other cultures; therefore definitions of sexual abuse and the response to sexual abuse may differ among America's diverse ethnic groups.

An incest offender's sense of ownership of his wife and children is a typical defense mechanism often seen with sex offenders, one that many probation/parole officers are familiar with confronting. However, if the incest offender is an Asian from Laos, it will be important to have knowledge of that offender's cultural belief system to more effectively work with his attitudes toward women and children. This does not mean that the behavior will be excused, only that knowledge of the offender's cultural belief system will improve the change process. In a Laotian family, the mother is expected to take a secondary role behind her husband which may have her appearing less protective of her daughter. Expressions of feelings may be more subdued, and there may be deep feelings of shame, guilt, and loss of face associated with admitting the abuse by the offender. As a result, the offender may resist repeating his admissions of guilt at later meetings (Okamura *et al.*, 1995). What may look like resistance may be more cultural, and the cultural differences may have the therapist or probation officer thinking that little progress is taking place when, in fact, progress is being made.

With recently arrived refugees it is helpful to be knowledgeable about their culture but also to address such issues as the intensity of trauma experienced before arriving in the United States, and whether they settled together or separated from other members of their culture. There were two refugee groups from Cambodia, the first in 1975 were fleeing the Khmer Rouge and were small in number; the second wave in the 1980s was large, and the refugees had experienced a decade of unimaginable trauma under the Khmer Rouge in which all evidence of normal life had been lost (Scully *et al.*, 1996). The first group had been "too widely disbursed to establish functioning communities and soon became overwhelmed by the stories of the new refugees who were giving accounts of those who had died" (Scully *et al.*, 1996). The chaos and trauma experienced by the Cambodian refugees under the Khmer Rouge has made adjustment extremely difficult, and responding adequately to the needs of both victim and perpetrator within that culture will require both sensitivity and knowledge of not only their culture but the traumatic historical past.

The subtle differences in various cultural mannerisms will have an impact on treatment and supervision, as well. Typically, many people are not aware of the meaning of patterns and customs different from their own. For example, eye contact has wide variations of meaning among cultures and easily can lead to misunderstandings. To many probation/parole officers, a sex offender who avoids eye contact is often regarded as dishonest or evasive. However, Puerto Rican men seldom look into each other's eyes and may regard direct eye contact as a challenge, and for Native Americans, direct eye contact is a show of disrespect. Furthermore, boundaries of space differ among cultures; Latinos generally stand closer when talking than North Americans who may regard physical closeness as threatening or even sexually motivated.

Certainly in a culture as diverse as ours, probation/parole officers must remain open to the reality that culture plays an important part in how a person responds to issues and situations in his or her life. Becoming knowledgeable of the multicultural diversity within your own community will help your supervision practices. The primary goal of supervision is community safety, and there are various routes to this goal. Part of community safety is engaging meaningfully with your client by becoming knowledgeable regarding multicultural diversity within your community and remaining sensitive to the subtle (and not so subtle) differences.

Juvenile Sex Offenders

Probation officers supervising adult sex offenders are more than likely to have some adolescent sex offenders on their caseloads. Although there are many similarities in the treatment and supervision of adult and adolescent sex offenders, there are also some significant differences.

Many of the treatment modalities of adult and adolescent treatment are the same; cognitive-behavioral strategies with the relapse prevention model are used by the majority of treatment providers working effectively with adolescent sex offenders (Freeman-Longo et al. 1994). The supervision strategies outlined in this manual also are relevant when supervising the adolescent sex offender.

The major difference has to do with the changing developmental needs of adolescent sex offenders. These developmental issues must be dealt with in conjunction with the treatment of the sexually abusive behavior. For the probation officer, this requires some knowledge of adolescent developmental issues. In the overall supervision planning, it will mean more involvement with the adolescent's caregiver such as parent, foster parent, group home, the school, and the adjunctive services that often are involved with high-risk adolescents.

A major issue is where the adolescent will live and the necessity for the caregiver to be involved in the treatment and supervision of the adolescent. Decisions as to whether the adolescent remains in the home must be addressed. For example, the adolescent may be appropriately placed in community treatment, but his home may be judged to be high risk due to the alcoholism of the father, the mother's refusal to believe her son committed the sexual offense, and/or the proximity of the victim's residence. A foster home may be a viable alternative in this case, but the foster home should have no other minor children residing in the home. Many foster homes, of course, have other children in the home so that placement of the adolescent sex offender is not always an easy one.

The treatment issues involved in placement will be the engagement of not only the foster parents but also the biological parents in the treatment process. The probation officer will need to include both the foster parents and the biological parents (if there is contact) in the supervising network.

The National Task Force on Juvenile Sexual Offending (National Council of Juvenile and Family Court Judges, 1993) recommended that placement options for adolescents be considered through a continuum of care model. This might include the following items:

Continuum of Care Placement Options for Adolescents

1. Short-term specialized psychoeducational programs for sexually abusive youths
2. Home-based supervision while attending specialized outpatient treatment
3. Foster-care homes where the foster parents are trained to manage sexually abusive youths while they attend specialized outpatient treatment in community-based programs
4. Residential group homes with staff trained to manage sexually abusive youths while they attend specialized outpatient treatment in community-based programs
5. Residential group treatment facilities with sex-offender specific treatment
6. Residential group homes with specialized day treatment for sexually abusive youths
7. Medium-security training schools with specialized treatment for sexually abusive youths
8. Secure residential treatment center (or secure group home) specially trained to manage and treat sexually abusive youths
9. Inpatient psychiatric hospital units with specialized treatment for sexually abusive youths
10. Maximum-security facility with specialized treatment for sexually abusive youths
11. Post-treatment support systems
12. Supervised apartments

Another issue in the supervision of the juvenile sex offender is the relationship with the school. Many school system personnel are not trained in the issues of sexual abuse, and this may present problems that range from enabling juvenile sex offenders to ostracizing them. The supervision issues to consider are the level of risk the adolescent may present to other students and the level of disclosure that should be made to the school regarding the offense history. It also will be necessary to consider the socialization and developmental needs of the adolescent in conjunction with considering the safety of the students and teachers. These are not easy issues. The team approach can be very helpful in making decisions so the probation officer is not making these decisions in isolation. With an adolescent, a school representative should be a member of the team.

Chapter 10

Teamwork

Because of the furtiveness of the sex offender's world, supervision is best accomplished by using a team concept as this allows greater insight into the offender's life than does the "snapshot" that individual supervision provides. The structure of team case management varies given the agencies involved and the available resources within each agency. Because of the probation/parole officers' mandate to control and manage the risk of the sex offender, they are generally the team case manager. Often, noncorrectional team members are not aware of the legal responsibilities of supervising offenders, or how the probation/parole officers' authority can be used to exert control over the offender's movements and support the treatment process.

Teams can be used for a variety of purposes in working with sex offenders. One team may be structured within the probation/parole office to collaborate on questions of supervision of specific offenders. Core members of this team are probation/parole officers and surveillance officers. They rely heavily on their own observations and the feedback they receive from sex-offender therapists, police, polygraphers, social workers, and network members to provide effective supervision with sex offenders.

A second team structure may focus primarily on treatment. For example, if an incest offender is reuniting with his family, a number of therapists may be involved in the reunification process. The probation/parole officer will be an important member of this team, providing information to the team from his or her field visits and collateral contacts, but he or she would typically not be the case manager. A third team may involve multiple agencies who are working with a mentally ill or intellectually disabled sex offender, and an individual will be designated team manager to coordinate and direct the process.

In general, team meetings should have a structured format, and be led by an individual with strong leadership skills. To achieve a constructive, full-functioning team, the questions in the box on the next page, relating to members' roles in the group and their relationships among one another, should be evaluated by the team manager.

Team supervision is a powerful tool in the monitoring of a sex offender's activities. However, the team must listen carefully to information being shared and present

Team Members

1. Members should be clear on their role within the team and with the information sharing process. Address any hierarchical arrangement within the group which inhibits sharing of information. Be conscious of individuals who feel restricted in the decision-making process such as the line worker who must pass all decisions by his or her supervisor. They should not be limited in their ability to provide appropriate information.

2. Team members should understand their larger role of community protection as well as rehabilitation of the offender. This common goal should be demonstrated in the treatment team process. Take note of individuals who manipulate information to gain a particular outcome such as allowing a risky offender to remain living in the community.

3. Be aware of undercurrents within the team, and note any conflict between team members. Is information being promptly disseminated? Do team members demonstrate reluctance to take on required tasks? Are the offenders engendering negative feelings from individuals on the team that are inhibiting the functioning of the team?

4. There should be equal opportunities for all team members to share information; that is, one team member's information is not routinely deemed more important than information from other members. Information from a therapist should not be seen as consistently more valuable than the probation/parole officer's observations of the sex offender in the community; both items are needed for a comprehensive treatment and supervision plan.

5. Use a mutually agreed upon format for how decisions are to be made, conveyed, and carried out within the team. Look for excessive time spent arguing points with no resolution or decisions made unilaterally with little team input.

6. Establish a protocol to provide feedback to the offender, and to other parties who have a need to receive information. Meetings must provide a balanced view of the sex offender's activities and the team should operate accordingly, seeking out both positive and negative aspects of the offender's progress.

7. Procedures must be in place to deal with conflict resolution and counterproductive behavior. Sex offenders can be masters at splitting people, and team members must remain vigilant to prevent this from occurring, not only among the team, but the adjunct network members as well.

a clear and objective picture of an offender's activities. They must understand the larger goal of long-term community safety and allow the offender the best opportunity for making positive changes.

Interagency Collaboration

Responding responsibly to child sexual abuse requires the cooperation of multiple agencies, ranging from child protection agencies, police, prosecutors, probation and parole, to mental health and substance-abuse professionals. This cooperation is essential if victims are to be treated humanely, offenders held accountable, and the community kept safe from further victimization.

The approach toward developing an interagency approach to child sexual abuse may vary from state to state or county to county, but the elements involved remain essentially the same. William Young (1988) outlined a typical protocol describing each agency's responsibilities:

1. All child sexual abuse reports should be jointly investigated by the child-protection agency and the police. This involves the social worker and the police investigating together. This joint interview not only reduces the number of times a victim is interviewed but allows for early collaboration between police and social services.

2. The prosecutor agrees to bring the substantiated cases to court immediately and to seek appropriate intervention from the judge. It is the court that can impose the special conditions of release following arraignment that can protect the victim and other potential victims from further victimization.

3. The child protection agency and the police are aware of treatment programs in their area so they can make appropriate referrals for the victim, nonoffending spouse, and the offender. The family almost certainly will be in a crisis, and gaining the cooperation of a family may best be done at this point.

4. The protocol should incorporate the philosophy that the offender should be the one to leave the home, not the victim. If the victim needs to be removed from the home because the nonoffending spouse is unable or unwilling to protect the victim, and there are other children in the home, the offender still should be required to leave. At this early stage, it is difficult to evaluate the risk the offender may pose to the other children. Until the completion of the psychosexual evaluation, sex offenders' visits with their other children should be supervised.

5. Involve all the agencies (such as social services, police, prosecutor, probation and parole) in the process by having them sign the protocol (see Addendum, page 137). Signing the protocol formalizes each agency's commitment and will help ensure that the protocol will be followed. Because of personnel changes and the need to periodically update protocols, the agencies should sign the protocol on a yearly basis. This also will help keep all the agencies aware of their responsibilities.

6. Sharing information among participants is essential. In some areas, the team members have been impaneled, which allows for free exchange of information during team meetings.

It is apparent from this protocol that specialized training regarding sex offenders and sexual abuse victims within the various agencies will be important to the success of any protocol. The need for sexual abuse issue specialists in each agency is paramount. Unfortunately, not all administrators believe philosophically in specialized units, and this may be a stumbling block.

All police officers, social workers, and probation/parole officers should receive training on sexual abuse issues. However, doing the actual work will involve a committed team which works well together and has a high level of trust for one another. For this reason, specialized teams are essential. Imagine a police department and a social service agency signing the protocol and sending a different officer and a different worker each time there is a report of sexual abuse. Imagine, too, the chaos for the prosecutor who has the specialized caseload having to potentially deal with a different police officer and a different social worker on each sexual abuse case. Imagine the phone messages that will go back and forth among these three agencies. It is not difficult to see the inefficiency that will quickly arise and the protracted time the cases will take to prosecute. Organizing units for consistency in handling cases is also strongly recommended.

Aside from the protocol, it is important to have a child protection team composed, at a minimum, of social workers, police, prosecutor, probation and parole officers, and treatment providers who meet monthly. In some areas, school guidance counselors also will be members of the team. Reviewing new cases and ongoing cases will be a focus of the meetings. The exchange of information is essential, so issues of confidentiality must be dealt with at the onset.

Law Enforcement Collaboration

It is critical to establish a working relationship with law enforcement agencies as they routinely observe offender activity which may be outside the purview of the probation/parole officer. To begin the process of collaboration, it is important to identify how each agency mutually can benefit the other and to define how information will be shared among entities. Become knowledgeable as to how those services are provided in your area. Note the following agencies when establishing collaborative relationships:

- state and local police agencies
- federal agencies (Federal Bureau of Investigation, Bureau of Alcohol Tobacco and Firearms, U.S. Marshal's Service, U.S. Postal Service Inspectors, the Immigration and Naturalization Service, and others)
- sheriff's offices
- specialized units (drug task force, violent crime and intelligence)

It is useful to address the following areas when establishing contact with law enforcement agencies:

1. **Identify a contact person at each probation, parole, and police department and maintain routine contact.**

Identify types of information you are seeking and learn the procedure to gain this information. For example, does the local police department have a computerized system that lists responses to complaints? Offenders may be involved in behaviors that do not result in criminal charges, such as the neighbor who called the police on the offender who was hanging around a schoolyard. This complaint may be documented in the law enforcement computer systems but would not automatically come to the attention of the probation/parole officer.

2. **Create a holding place for information and composites related to sexual offenses.**

When looking for suspects, police departments frequently share among agencies composites of suspects with descriptive information. Having a place to post and maintain this information for routine review by probation/parole staff increases the possibility of apprehension of the offender.

3. **Send offender identification, photos, and special conditions of probation/parole to the local law enforcement agency.**

Law enforcement officers need to know which sex offenders are in the community and their conditions of probation/parole. If an offender begins to engage in high-risk behavior, the probation/parole officer then could be notified. Consider the case of a woman who was sexually assaulted in the parking lot of a popular night spot.

> The victim alleged the perpetrator had distinctive facial features and was wearing his hair in a particular style. The officer reviewed the file of photos of sex offenders received from the probation office. Based on the victim's description and a photograph on file that matched the description, the police officer made a quick apprehension of a suspect who was eventually convicted of the crime.

4. **Collaborate with law enforcement around technical violations.**

A police officer often encounters an offender engaged in noncriminal but high-risk conduct. The probation/parole officer may be able to effect a response that a police officer could not if the behavior is a violation of the offender's probation conditions. For example, a police officer may respond to a complaint of a man photographing children at a playground. The man is not touching the children, only engaging them in conversation as he takes their pictures. A record check shows the man to be on probation for sexual assault of a minor. The photographing and talking to the children is not a criminal act, but it is a violation of the offender's parole to be in the presence of minor children. The parole officer could implement a number of sanctions while the police would be powerless in the situation.

5. **Participate in law enforcement intelligence briefings when appropriate.**
A designated probation/parole officer or supervisor should be part of these briefings. If there is a task force developed to address issues of sexual abuse, the probation/ parole departments should have a representative.

6. **Invite law enforcement agencies to specialized departmental training, and reciprocate by attending law enforcement training, where applicable.**
Many law enforcement agencies provide training on drug identification information, verbal communications skills, and other areas. Conversely, correctional agencies may offer training that would be beneficial to law enforcement. For example, training regarding the cycle of violence in domestic abuse or the relapse prevention model would be of benefit to law enforcement agencies, particularly those with specialized units.

7. **Offer assistance where appropriate to foster good working relationships.**
Tasks as simple as hand carrying paperwork to a police investigator or running an offender's name through the computer system to provide an updated address could be of enormous benefit to a law enforcement agency. Learning your way around local police agencies and developing a first-name relationship with law enforcement officers enhances the working relationship and can build mutual respect.

8. **Establish good working relationships with individuals handling records at various law enforcement sites.**
The ability to obtain information through the records department of a law enforcement agency is often critical for a probation/parole officer. Familiarization with the agency's process for securing information as well as providing enough lead time for the agency to search for information is important.

9. **Show appreciation for the work of law enforcement.**
In a world where everyone is asked to do more with less, law enforcement agencies work with a difficult clientele and receive few accolades. It is important to positively recognize the work of individuals within the agencies we depend on and continue to build the collaborative relationships that will enable us to function more smoothly.

Preventing Burnout

Gary Cornelius (1994) explains burnout as "unrelieved work stress, long-term involvement in demanding situations, and continuous, intense stress." Burnout is an occupational hazard when working with an offender population. Samenow (1984) stated that more serious than physical attack in working with an offender population was the rapid burnout of enthusiasm, commitment, and interest. Those working with offender populations often become overwhelmed, not only by the risk presented, but by some of the realities often inherent in the job. Those realities translate into burgeoning caseloads, reduced budgets, increased paperwork demands, liability issues, political agendas, and conflicting roles with courts, law enforcement, district attorneys, and defense attorneys.

Providing effective supervision for sex offenders requires a level of skill and proficiency acquired from experience, training, observation, successes, and, yes, some mistakes. However, that level of effectiveness does not come without some costs, and often that cost is increased lack of motivation on the part of the officer, or put quite simply: "burnout." Samenow (1984) also describes officers blaming their lack of experience for offenders' relapse or doubting their suitability for the work. More commonly, however, officers may begin to resent offenders, doubting their capability to make a positive change. At this point, superficial, cynical supervision of the sex offender may replace energetic, effective, and resilient supervision.

Sex offenders remain on supervision longer than many other types of offenders, due to the high-risk nature of their behaviors and the often lengthy sentences they receive. Therefore, sex offender casework may become tedious and draining due to the frequent contact and constant vigilance required. No probation or parole officer, however, must or should endure the stresses of this job unaided or alone.

There are, in fact, two methods which can forestall or eliminate burnout without compromising the quality of supervision. The first strategy to consider is teamwork. The input of others may enable both you and the offender to gain important new perspectives which will lead to fresh, effective methods of supervision. The team dynamic improves the chance, for example, that a sex offender's high-risk behaviors, often difficult to detect in a long-term one-on-one supervision, may be more readily detected and confronted.

Use of the team also reduces the feeling of isolation that may come when one must make decisions and, at times, initiate legal action that could result in long-term incarceration due to an offender's behavior. Certainly, teamwork concerning these crucial interventions enhances the probability that the course of action will be effective. It provides a check and balance of the system and reduces the effect of personalizing the decision when the court or parole board goes against the team recommendation. The team offers support for rethinking and maintaining the energy and confidence that are vital for working effectively.

The camaraderie of teamwork also encourages a sense of humor that, in turn, provides the likelihood of renewal and fresh perspective. And when the work goes well, the feeling of reward and accomplishment is intensified and validated by having shared the process of supervision with one's colleagues.

A second strategy for consideration is the intra-office transfer. At times, the inclusion of team members into your work with an offender may not be enough to provide the healthy renewal and productive functioning you are after—both for yourself and the offender. The reasons vary, of course. At such times, the responsible professional decision may be to disengage, transferring the offender's case to another experienced officer. In doing so, the officer gains a respite, and the offender must revisit his or her offense and relapse pattern with the new officer. In doing so, missed territory may be found, fresh insight gained, and any dulled vision that may have set in with the offender due to familiarity and routine can be cleared.

We offer one final observation about confronting and coping with burnout that is vital. Regardless of the helpfulness of the strategies for overcoming burnout, success in defeating its disheartening and debilitating effects rests with each individual. Each of us must explore which coping strategies will serve us best as we take action to ensure that our health and professional competence remain intact or are restored.

Rather than simply reacting to the ravages of burnout in an instinctual or scattered way, it is essential that we take positive steps to overcome the emotional, physical, and spiritual depletion that burnout brings. We must discover what works for us, such as exercise, meditation, teamwork, or counseling. Then we must take action. The responsibility is ours. The good news is that, ultimately, we are our own best allies. The know-how and guidance we offer others surely can be put to the service of ourselves.

Conclusion

Our handbook intends to provide officers who do the day-to-day work with sex offenders with information and strategies useful in establishing a framework for effective, safe sex-offender supervision. We hope officers will use the information this book provides by adapting our procedures and suggestions to their unique jurisdictions. Use this handbook as a tool for making changes in supervision practice, staffing patterns, or case assignments.

Competent, successful sex-offender supervision often begins, we believe, with line staff who are motivated to gain expertise in working with sex offenders. We offer the following suggestions for beginning, or for reshaping, whatever practices are currently in place.

First, assess your offender caseload. There may be sex offenders already in the community who are high risk and need the structure recommended.

Second, if you have an incarcerated sex-offender treatment program, you may chose to apply our supervision model to the offenders released back into the community.

Third, if you have identified a therapist who does group work with sex offenders, you may offer to help set up a supervision team, or network, for the sex offenders in his or her group.

Further along, as staff become more skilled and treatment well established, the scope of supervision within the office can be increased.

Remember: sex offenses are not impulsive, uncontrollable events. Sex offenders can change. Our charge is to create an atmosphere in which positive change can occur and to provide the tools with which the sex offender can make those changes. For those offenders who chose not to control their harmful behaviors, we need to take actions that will hold them accountable and to provide consequences that will ultimately protect the community.

Addendum

Glossary

ABSTINENCE: The decision to refrain from taking part in a self-prohibited behavior. For sex offenders, abstinence is marked by the absence of fantasies, thought, materials, and behaviors that are associated with their offense patterns.

ABSTINENCE VIOLATION EFFECT (AVE): A term used to describe a variety of changes in beliefs and behaviors that can result from engaging in a lapse. Among the components of the AVE are a sense that treatment was a failure, or attributing the lapse to being weak-willed and unable to create personal change. Other components of AVE are not anticipating that lapses will occur or recalling only the positive aspects of the abusive behavior (also referred to as the Problem of Immediate Gratification). When sex offenders are not prepared to cope with the AVE, the likelihood of relapse increases. The AVE is experienced most strongly when clients believe that lapses should never occur.

ADAPTIVE COPING RESPONSE: A change in thoughts, feelings, or behaviors that effectively deals with a risk factor or lapse and reduces the likelihood of relapse. Adaptive coping responses may be either general or situationally specific. An example is the offender calling his AA sponsor if he is having the urge to drink.

AGGRAVATING CIRCUMSTANCES: Conditions that intensify the seriousness of the sex offense. Conditions may include age, reduced physical and/or mental capacity of the victim, the level of cruelty used to perpetrate the offense, the presence of a weapon during the commission of the offense, denial of responsibility, multiple victims, degree of planning, history of related conduct on the part of the offender, use of position of status or trust to perpetrate the offense.

ALFORD PLEA: This allows the offender to admit that there is enough evidence to convict him or her at trial without admitting to the offense of record. This type of plea often precludes treatment since it is difficult to treat someone who claims not to have a problem.

CHILD MOLESTER: Any male or female who engages in illegal sexual activity with children.

COGNITIVE DISTORTION: A thinking error or rationalization that is used by sex offenders to justify abusive emotions and behaviors. In essence, these are self-generated excuses for taking part in one's relapse patterns.

COLLATERAL CONTACTS: Contacts made by staff charged with offender supervision that are auxiliary to traditional supervision techniques. Use of collateral information enhances the quality of supervision and will include contacts with law enforcement, employers, family, and friends of the offender. A variety of individuals in the community may have information to share that will be both supportive and/or informative of potential high-risk behavior.

DISPOSITION: A final settlement of criminal charges.

DISINHIBITORS: Internal or external stimuli which decrease personal prohibitions against engaging in sex offenses. One example of an internal disinhibitor is a cognitive distortion ("That eight-year old sure is leering at me"). Substance use is another example of an external disinhibitor.

EXTERNAL SUPERVISORY DIMENSION (ESD): The aspect of relapse prevention that enhances the ability of probation/parole officers and significant others (such as employer, family, friends) to monitor a sex offender's offense precursors.

INTERNAL SELF-MANAGEMENT DIMENSION (ISD): The aspect of relapse prevention that allows a sex offender to better recognize and control offense precursors.

LAPSE: An emotion, fantasy, thought, or behavior that is part of an offender's relapse patterns. Lapses are not sex offenses but are precursors or risk factors for sex offenses.

MALADAPTIVE COPING RESPONSES: An apparent effort to deal with a risk factor or lapse that actually enables the sex offender to get closer to relapse. For example, an angry rapist who decides to take a drive in order to cool off might decide to stop at a bar for a drink.

MITIGATING CIRCUMSTANCES: Conditions that may modify the seriousness of the sex offense. Conditions may include the offender participating in the offense under coercion or duress, lack of sufficient capacity on the part of the offender for judgment due to physical or mental impairment, sincere remorse and a course of action undertaken to demonstrate restitution, responsibility, culpability. Extreme caution should be taken when looking at mitigating circumstances with sex offenders. Often such factors can be viewed as excusing the perpetrator for his or her actions, while discounting the trauma upon the victim.

NOLO CONTENDERE: A defendant may plead *nolo contendere* only with the consent of the court after the judge has obtained a factual basis. A conviction based on a plea of *nolo contendere* is admissible in evidence for all purposes for which a conviction based on a plea of guilty is admissible. A plea of *nolo contendere* cannot be considered an admission of guilt in civil court proceedings.

PARAPHILIA: Psychosexual disorder. Some examples of paraphilia are the following: pedophilia, exhibitionism, fetishism, and voyeurism.

PEDOPHILIA: The Diagnostic and Statistical Manual of Mental Disorders (DSM-IV) criteria for pedophilia is as follows: A) over a period of at least six months, recurrent, intense sexually arousing fantasies, sexual urges, or behaviors involving sexual activity with a prepubescent child or children (generally age thirteen years or younger); B) the fantasies, sexual urges or behaviors cause clinically significant distress or impairment in social, occupational, or other important areas of functioning; C) the person is at least age sixteen years and at least five years older than the child or children in Criterion A. (Do not include an individual in late adolescence involved in an ongoing sexual relationship with a twelve or thirteen year old). This is a diagnostic definition. In recent years, many professionals have used this term interchangeably with child molester, resulting in some confusion.

PENILE PLETHYSMOGRAPH: A device used to measure the erectile responses in males and record their arousal patterns to deviant and nondeviant sexual stimuli.

PRECURSORS: A general term used to encompass seemingly unimportant decisions (SUDs), maladaptive coping responses, risk factors, lapses, and the abstinence violation effect. Precursors are events that occur prior to a sex offense.

PRESENTENCE INVESTIGATION REPORT: A court-ordered report prepared by a probation officer. This report includes information about the defendant's offense of record, criminal record, family and personal history, employment and financial history, substance-abuse history, and prior periods of probation supervision and/or incarceration. At the conclusion of the report, the probation officer assesses the information and makes a recommendation to the court as to disposition.

PROBLEM OF IMMEDIATE GRATIFICATION (PIG phenomenon): The PIG phenomenon is part of the Abstinence Violation Effect (AVE). It occurs when sex offenders selectively remember the positive sensations experienced during, or immediately after, past assaults. Recalling only the immediate positive sensations from past assaults increases the likelihood of another offense. The problem of immediate gratification is that the offenders forget about the negative consequences that generally are delayed (such as guilt, loss of family and friends, loss of employment, newspaper and television coverage of arrest and conviction, incarceration, parole). When offenders learn to counter the strength of the PIG phenomenon by focusing on the delayed negative effects of their acts (and the immediate and delayed harmful impacts on victims), the likelihood of relapse decreases.

RELAPSE: A sexual abusive behavior or sexual offense.

RELAPSE PREVENTION (RP): A process for enhancing emotional, cognitive, and behavioral self-management and external supervision of sex offenders.

RISK CONTROL: Conditions placed on an offender to inhibit reoffense. Conditions may include levels of supervision, surveillance, or incarceration. In a community setting, specialized protection/parole conditions are imposed and carried out by staff charged with overseeing the offender's placement in the community.

RISK FACTORS: A set of internal stimuli or external circumstances that threaten a sex offender's self-control and thus increase the risk of lapse or relapse.

RISK MANAGEMENT: Term used to describe services provided by corrections departments to manage the risk presented by offenders. Services may include surveillance of offenders in a community setting (risk control) and the requirement to participate in rehabilitative activities (risk reduction).

RISK REDUCTION: Activities designed to address the risk factors contributing to the offender's sexually deviant behaviors. These activities will be rehabilitative in nature and provide the offender with the necessary knowledge, skills, and attitudes to reduce likelihood of reoffense.

SELF-DEPRECATION: Belittling or putting down oneself.

SEEMINGLY UNIMPORTANT DECISIONS (SUDs): Decisions that seem to have little bearing on whether a lapse or relapse will occur, but which actually allow the offender to get closer to or further away from high-risk factors that increase the probability of another offense. A pedophile who decides to go to a family-oriented movie on a Saturday afternoon is making a Seemingly Unimportant Decision. The inevitable presence of children at the theater allows the offender to place himself in a high-risk situation where he may lapse or relapse.

STIMULUS CONTROL: A specific coping response that removes from an offender's daily environment all items associated with that person's relapse pattern. As an example, a pedophile who views child erotica to enhance sexual fantasies can remove all photographs and drawings of children from his home and office. Specialized conditions of probation/parole are the external component of stimulus control.

VICTIM-IMPACT STATEMENT: Statement taken while interviewing the victim during the course of the presentence investigation report. The purpose is to discuss the impact the sexual offense has had on the victim.

Suggested Probation and Parole Conditions

Programming/Treatment

___ You shall successfully enroll, participate in, and complete a program for sex offenders approved by your probation/parole officer and assume the costs of your treatment.

___ You shall allow your sex offender treatment provider unrestricted communication with your probation/parole officer regarding your attendance, level of participation, and any other information deemed necessary to protect the community from your sexually abusive behavior.

___ You shall maintain use of prescribed medications.

Victim Contact

___ You shall assume the financial costs for the therapy of your victim(s).

___ You may not have any contact with your victim(s) (including letters, phone calls, tapes, videos, visits, or any form of contact through a third party) until approved by your therapist, your victim (the victim's parents if the victim is a child), your victim's therapist, and your probation/parole officer.

___ You (as an incest offender) may not have visitation with the victim unless approved by your therapist, your victim, your victim's therapist, the child protective services worker, and your probation/parole officer.

___ You (as an incest offender) may not have contact with your nonvictim children unless approved by your therapist, child protection worker, and probation/parole officer.

Offense-specific

___ You may not view videotapes, films, or television shows that act as a stimulus for your abusive cycle, or act as a stimulus to arouse you in an abusive fashion, in other words, a pedophile may not view shows whose primary character is a child.

___ You may not use pornography or erotica: you may not frequent adult bookstores, sex shops, topless bars, or massage parlors.

___ You may not frequent places where children congregate, such as parks, playgrounds, and schools.

___ If you have photographed your victim(s) in the past, you may not possess a camera or video recorder.

Alcohol and Drug Use and Abuse

___ You shall submit to alcosensor/urinalysis at the direction of your probation/parole officer.

__ You may not purchase, consume, or possess alcohol and/or illegal substances.

__ You may not frequent bars, taverns, and businesses whose primary functions is to serve alcoholic beverages.

__ You shall not associate with known alcohol and drug users without prior permission of your probation/parole officer.

__ You will attend and successfully complete an alcohol- and/or drug-treatment program.

Monitoring

__ You are required to meet with your probation/parole officer as directed.

__ You are required to give your probation/parole officer search and seizure privileges to confiscate drugs, pornography, and/or erotica.

__ You must maintain a daily log (including such items as daily activities, fantasies, and so on).

__ You must agree to a polygraph examination to determine your involvement in criminal sexual activity and/or risk factors for sexual abuse. These examinations will be periodic upon therapist's or probation/parole officer's request.

__ You must participate in a plethysmograph examination to determine your sexual arousal to abusive themes. These examinations will be periodic upon the therapist's or probation/parole officer's request.

__ You must observe curfew restrictions as directed by your probation/parole officer.

Social

__ You may not associate with felons unless they are in treatment with you and the therapist and probation/parole officer approve of the affiliation.

__ You shall inform all persons with whom you have a significant relationship or close affiliation of your sexual offending history. The therapist and/or probation/parole officer will determine who shall be informed.

__ You may not participate in friendships or relationships with women who have children.

__ You may not have contact with male or female persons under the age of eighteen unless accompanied by a responsible adult (approved by your therapist and probation/parole officer) who is aware of your patterns of sexual abuse.

__ You may not socialize with individuals under the age of sixteen in work or social situations unless accompanied by a responsible adult (approved by your therapist and probation/parole officer) who is aware of your patterns of sexual abuse.

__ You may not engage in activities that will bring you into close contact with children.

__ You will not live in an apartment complex that allows children, in neighborhoods with large numbers of children, or in neighborhoods near parks, schools, and playgrounds.

Driving

__ You must maintain a driving log (mileage; time of departure, arrival, and return; destination; routes traveled; persons with you).

__ You may not pick up hitchhikers or hitchhike yourself.

__ You must comply with specified limitations on driving, such as not driving after dark, not driving alone, not driving at specified times, or not driving with female passengers, depending on your individual criminal history and offense patterns.

__ You may not drive alone with a single female unless there is a specific reason, for example, a prearranged date whose name, address, and phone number you have reported to your probation/parole officer and therapist.

General

__ You must reside in a residence approved by your probation/parole officer.

__ You must maintain full-time school and/or employment.

__ Your employment must be approved by your probation/parole officer.

__ You may not purchase or possess firearms.

__ Other_____

_____

__ Other_____

_____

__ Other_____

_____

__ Other_____

_____

_____

Client   Date

_____

Probation/Parole Officer   Date

Sample-Letter to Law Enforcement for Travel Purposes

Date:

Dear Law Enforcement Professional:

_____ is on probation for charges of _____.
He is required to present this letter to a Law Enforcement professional whenever traveling to a destination outside of Vermont.

The purpose of this information is to provide notification to you that he is staying in the area and has a past history of _____.

This letter is not intended to warn you that this offender is a high risk for reoffending since he would not be approved for out-of-state travel if this were the case. Rather, it is intended as a general deterrent for the offender as well as a way in which he can hold himself accountable to local authorities and our program. Fulfilling responsibilities such as this one is an essential part of an offender's treatment while in the community.

The offender bringing this letter is fully aware of its contents and is prepared to discuss any issues which you feel are necessary to his safe conduct in your jurisdiction. We encourage you to ask the offender a little more about himself if he does not offer to do so. We would also appreciate your signing and dating this letter so that this offender can verify that he has fulfilled his responsibility when he returns to Vermont.

Please feel free to phone our office if you have any questions regarding this procedure.

Sincerely,

Probation/Parole Officer

Name of Law Enforcement Official (please print) _____

Signature of Law Enforcement Official: _____

Position and Agency: _____

Address and Phone Number: _____

Date Signed: _____

Acknowledgment of Limited Confidentiality and Waiver

I,_____, have been informed and acknowledge that I have limited rights of confidentiality regarding my treatment at the _____(agency)_____.

I understand that the purposes of this waiver are for coordinating and planning my treatment, protecting the community from my sexually aggressive behavior, and repairing damage perpetrated on my victims by my sexually aggressive and other abusive behavior.

I consent to unrestricted communication between the treatment staff at the _____(agency)_____ and the Department of Corrections personnel responsible for my supervision. I also consent to unrestricted communication between treatment staff and any other individual or agency with whom treatment staff judge communication is necessary to achieve the purposes stated above. I understand that these individuals or agencies may include, but are not limited to, the court, the victim, and Social and Rehabilitation Services.

I also understand that treatment staff are obligated under Vermont law to report acts of abuse towards children, the disabled, and the elderly. There is also a general obligation of treatment staff to inform the authorities or others if, in the professional opinion of staff, my behavior presents a clear and imminent danger to either myself or other persons.

I understand that sexually aggressive behavior is criminal conduct that has serious consequences to the victim and the community. I want to control my sexually aggressive behavior, and I wish to be held fully accountable for my behavior.

I acknowledge that this waiver is signed without threat, promise, or coercion and is a voluntary act on my part.

_____   _____
Signature of Client   Date

_____   _____
Witness   Date

_____   _____
Witness   Date

(Printed with the permission of Robert McGrath)

Sex-offender Treatment Agreement

I,_____, hereby enter into this Treatment
Contract with the _____(agency)_____, to allow their staff
to provide me with treatment services for my sexually aggressive behavior. I understand
that the four primary goals of treatment are: (1) to help me reduce my risk to reoffend;
(2) to protect the community from my sexually aggressive behavior; (3) to help repair
damage perpetrated on my victims by my sexually aggressive and other abusive behavior; (4) to help incest families reunify when it is in the best interest of the victim.

1. I agree to be honest and assume full responsibility for my offense(s) and my
   behavior. I understand that successful treatment depends upon full acknowledgment of my offense(s), regardless of my plea in court (i.e., *nolo* or Alford).
2. I agree, if and when it is deemed appropriate by treatment staff, to make a clarification to my victim(s) of my responsibility for the sexual abuse.
3. I agree to sign an acknowledgment of limited confidentiality and waiver and to sign
   any releases of information required to obtain information about my behavior.
4. I will attend all treatment sessions and attend on time. I understand that the only
   acceptable excuse for absence or lateness is a verifiable medical or other personal
   emergency. I will notify the appropriate staff member as soon as possible about
   any situation that affects my attendance or promptness.
5. I will pay my assigned fee at the time of each session unless I have made other
   arrangements with the staff.
6. I will not engage in the illegal use of alcohol or other drugs or use alcohol or
   drugs to the extent that it interferes with my employment or the welfare of my
   family, others, or myself. I agree to submit to alcosensor and urinalysis testing as
   requested by treatment staff. I will not purchase, possess, or use sexually stimulating materials of any kind as defined by my treatment staff. I will not become
   verbally threatening or assaultive toward any staff member or client either inside
   or outside the office. I will advise treatment staff of any change in my residence
   or employment status.
7. I will not disclose any information regarding another client to anyone outside
   this program. I agree to have no contact with other sex offenders outside my
   treatment group without prior approval of treatment staff. I will keep treatment
   staff informed of the nature of any contact I have with another client outside the
   treatment sessions.
8. I will actively participate in treatment. I understand that treatment typically consists of weekly group therapy and may include periodic individual, couples, and
   family therapy sessions. Treatment generally can be expected to last an average
   of two years followed by approximately one year of periodic aftercare meetings.

I understand that my treatment will focus on seven areas: (1) accepting responsibility for my offense behaviors; (2) developing a supervision network of carefully selected family and/or friends who can help me with my recovery; (3) changing thinking patterns that contributed to my offenses; (4) developing empathy for my victims and others; (5) controlling my sexual arousal patterns; (6) improving social skills related to my offending behavior such as anger management, conflict resolution, self-esteem, alcohol and drug abuse, and stress management; and (7) developing relapse-prevention skills by identifying and learning how to avoid high-risk situations and intervening in my offense cycle.

I understand that treatment techniques that will be used in the program include talk therapy, writing, reading, watching films, hearing lectures, role-playing, and participating in discussions. I understand that I may be asked to discuss my treatment progress and treatment assignments in group treatment, with my probation/parole officer, and other significant adults in my life. I understand that treatment will include aversive conditioning, which is a procedure that pairs deviant sexual thoughts with aversive elements. Aversive elements may include noxious scenes, boredom, and noxious odors. I understand that I may be asked to engage in masturbation in the privacy of my own home for treatment purposes.

9. I understand that my offense behavior has had an impact on my living partners. To help my living partners and myself in the recovery process, I will actively encourage my current partners, or any future significant living partners, to participate in treatment on an as-needed basis as determined by treatment staff.

10. I understand that ongoing assessment of my progress through psychological and physiological evaluation (penile plethysmograph and clinical polygraph) may be part of my treatment.

11. I understand that treatment involves certain risks, and I have discussed these with treatment staff. For example, discussing possibly embarrassing personal issues in treatment, undergoing physiological evaluations, and completing aversive conditioning may cause me to feel anxious, nervous, upset, angry, guilty, ashamed, or depressed. Discussion of treatment assignments with my family and significant others may place stress on my relationships with these individuals. I will inform staff if I experience undue stress as a result of any treatment intervention and understand treatment will be available if any such symptoms should persist.

12. I understand that I have the right and will have the opportunity to have each treatment method explained to me before being requested to carry out each new treatment method. I understand that I have the right to refuse to participate in any assessment or treatment method. I also understand that if I refuse to participate in one or more assessment or treatment methods, that I may become ineligible for continued treatment.

13. I understand that treatment staff may provide periodic verbal and written reports to Probation and Parole and other individuals and agencies involved in my treatment. I understand that the information in reports provided by treatment staff may influence the court's decisions regarding modifications or revocation of existing court orders.

14. I am aware that the practice of mental health treatment is not an exact science, and I acknowledge that no guarantees have been made to me about the results of assessments and treatment. I understand that some recent research suggests that the prospects of controlling my sexually deviant behavior may be increased by my enrollment in and successful completion of a specialized sex-offender treatment program.

15. I acknowledge that I have been provided with information about programs that would be alternatives to this sex offender treatment program.

16. I agree to avoid situations and behaviors that will place me at high risk of reoffending. I also agree to provide staff with a weekly "contact log" that details any accidental, incidental, or intentional contact that I have had with potential victims.

17. I agree to abide by the following special conditions:

_____

_____

18. I understand that my probation/parole officer may be notified of any violation of this agreement. I also understand that local or state police departments may be contacted, if necessary, to maintain victim or community safety. I also understand and agree that any violation of the conditions of this agreement may be grounds for termination from the program at the discretion of the staff. I agree that the staff may terminate my treatment for any other problem behavior not outlined above.

19. I understand that a staff member is on call for emergencies on a twenty-four (24) hour basis by calling (000-0000).

I have read, understand, and acknowledge that I am required to follow all the conditions listed above regarding my treatment and behavior. If I have any questions about this treatment agreement, I have discussed them to my satisfaction with the person in charge of my treatment. By signing this treatment agreement, I give voluntary consent to participate in all the above.

Signed:_____   Date:_____

Witnessed:_____   Date:_____

Witnessed:_____   Date:_____

(Reprinted with permission of Robert McGrath)

Psychosexual Evaluation Agreement

I, _____, hereby enter into this Psychosexual Evaluation Agreement with the _____ (agency)_____ to allow their staff to provide me with psychosexual evaluation services. The purpose of the evaluation is

_____

_____

1. I understand that the fee for my psychosexual evaluation, including a written report, is _____, and is due on or before the date of the evaluation, or the evaluation will not commence. If payment for the evaluation is guaranteed by a governmental or social service agency, then payment may be postponed until after completion of the evaluation.
2. I understand that my first evaluation appointment is scheduled for _____ and will be conducted at _____.
3. I understand that an administrative fee of _____ will be charged if I cancel my scheduled evaluation within _____ working days of the date reserved. I understand that the guarantor(s) of the evaluation will be so charged, unless the guarantor is a governmental or social agency, in which case, I will be so charged.
4. I understand that I may refuse to participate in any or all aspects of my evaluation. I further understand that failure to fully participate in and complete my evaluation will jeopardize the evaluation process and staff may terminate the evaluation and/or may not be able to render an opinion or report.
5. I understand that the results of my evaluation may be written in a report and that this report may be sent to _____

_____.

   I further understand that evaluation staff may testify about the results of my evaluation in court.
6. I understand that there are other limits to confidentiality in the evaluation process and that evaluation staff are obligated under Vermont law to report acts of abuse towards children, the disabled, and the elderly. There is also a general obligation of the _____ to inform the authorities or others, if in the professional opinion of the staff, my behavior presents a clear and imminent danger to either myself or others.
7. I understand that evaluation staff do not have a duty or obligation to represent me in a court of law in regard to this evaluation. A court appearance may require an additional agreement and an additional fee.
8. I understand that this is an agreement for evaluation only and does not constitute any type of decision regarding counseling or acceptance into treatment at the _____.

9. I understand that my evaluation may include any or all of the following evaluation components:

A. Background information—The referring individual or agency should arrange to have relevant records (such as psychological evaluations, major hospitalization records, victim statements, police affidavits, etc.) forwarded to the _____ so that they may be reviewed prior to my evaluation. I understand that I may be asked to sign releases to obtain other information about my history and that evaluation staff may want to interview other individuals relevant to my case.

B. Psychological Testing—During this portion of the evaluation, I will be asked to complete paper-and-pencil tests that will assess such areas as my personality characteristics, intellectual abilities, and sexual knowledge, attitudes, and behavior. This portion of the evaluation typically takes two-to-four hours. I understand that if I have difficulty reading, test items will be read to me.

C. Psychophysiological Testing—During this portion of the evaluation, I will be asked to sit alone in a room and either watch and/or listen to stimuli depicting sexual scenes. While I am attending to these stimuli, I will be wearing a small gauge that I have placed on my penis. This gauge is connected to a machine in a nearby room. This machine will allow the evaluator to identify the extent to which I have sexual interest in each of the stimuli presented and to determine the types of activity that I find most sexually interesting. This procedure typically takes between one and two hours.

D. Clinical Interview—During this portion of the evaluation, I will be asked to discuss important events that have occurred during my life. I may be asked questions about my parents, educational background, hobbies, sexual development, substance abuse, and other topics. This portion of the evaluation typically takes two-to-four hours.

10. I understand that discussion and assessment of possibly embarrassing personal issues during the evaluation may cause me to feel anxious, angry, or depressed. If any such symptoms should persist, I understand that evaluation staff can arrange to provide me treatment for these symptoms.

I/We understand and accept this evaluation agreement.

_____   _____
Signature of Client   Date

_____   _____
Signature of Parent, Guardian, or Legal   Date
Representative

_____   _____
Witness to Signature(s)   Date

(Reprinted with permission of Robert McGrath)

Child Sexual Abuse Protocol

I. Introduction and Definitions

A. This protocol has been developed as a cooperative effort by concerned agencies and individuals in _____ County. The purpose of the protocol is to help personnel from various disciplines recognize and respond appropriately to children who have been sexually abused, to their families, and to the perpetrator of the sexual abuse.

B. For the purposes of this protocol, sexual abuse of children consists of any act or acts of any person involving sexual molestation or sexual exploitation of a child including _____ (insert your state statutes)_____ .

II. Guidelines for Reporting and Responding to Child Sexual Abuse Cases

The following is intended as a brief description of the reporting process and response to suspected or confirmed cases of child sexual abuse. More detailed protocols for each organization or agency may be developed by individual agencies for use by their own workers and, if so, are available on request.

A. Reporting

Social Services is the State agency mandated by law to deal with suspected or confirmed cases of child sexual abuse. In any case of child sexual abuse, Social Services must be notified. _____(insert state law)_____

Upon receipt of a report of child sexual abuse, Social Services will, in accordance with State law and department policy, assign a social worker to investigate the report within seventy-two hours. If the report constitutes an emergency, it will be investigated immediately.

The social worker assigned to the case will be responsible for ensuring that the Law Enforcement Agency is notified and will make arrangements to conduct a joint investigation. This will usually take the form of the initial face-to-face contact being made by the social worker and the police investigator together. Following the joint interview with the alleged victim, the police will continue the investigation and will make the appropriate contact with the district attorney's office. Social Services will also send a written report of the initial report to the district attorney's office with a copy to the police.

In sexual abuse investigations in which the police are involved prior to Social Services intervention, the police will promptly report the facts of their investigation to Social Services and the district attorney's office. It is assumed that in cases of a violent, life-threatening assault, or where an assault is in progress, the police may be the first called. The police agency in these situations is responsible for immediately ensuring that Social Services also has the information.

The investigation of the alleged sex offender shall be conducted by the police. The Social Services investigation and initial interviews shall focus on the child victim(s) and other nonoffending family members. If the alleged offender is a family member, Social Services shall not interrogate him/her but will record any information or admission that is voluntarily given. If the Social Services worker does receive this information, any statements made may be used in court.

The Social Services workers shall not give legal advice to the alleged offender nor shall they make statements about the police investigation other than the fact that there may be one. It is expected that in most situations, the police investigator will be present and will address these issues with the alleged offender. During joint investigations and interviews, the police officer and the Social Services worker should be working in a cooperative manner that complements each other's roles and, in that capacity, should be helpful to one another. This does not imply that their roles are the same. While the primary goal of both is to protect the child, the police officer remains concerned with the investigation of criminal activity; the Social Services worker with such issues as victim safety, family dynamics, and treatment.

If the alleged offender is a minor at the time of the offense, Social Services will treat this young person as an alleged offender and will refer the matter to the appropriate police department for investigation.

B. Responsibilities

1. Social Services:

Social Services has responsibility for the initial investigation and protection of the child. This typically will be done in conjunction with the police investigator. The social worker focuses on a determination regarding the facts of the abuse and establishing what environment will afford further protection for the child if abuse is established. Social Services will also check with Probation/Parole regarding the alleged offender's history with that department.

Social Services may make recommendations to the district attorney regarding conditions of release for the offender when criminal charges are brought, and it is anticipated that Social Services, the police, and the district attorney's office will cooperate with each other when there is doubt as to the appropriateness of criminal charges.

Social Services prepares the family court case, if any, and may make recommendations to the district attorney regarding sentencing disposition in the criminal cases.

Social Services works with the family to establish concrete goals, monitor progress, and makes decisions and recommendations regarding the reconstitution of the family. In making these recommendations and in monitoring progress, Social Services will routinely consult with the mental health professionals involved with the family, the probation/parole officer, and the Child Sexual Abuse Response Team. The district attorney's office will be informed as to who the mental health professionals are and the reunification plan.

In cases of child sexual abuse within a family setting, the perpetrator will typically be asked (or ordered by the court) to leave the home the day the abuse is substantiated. This is done to protect the victim(s) from further victimization and to facilitate treatment for all concerned. In situations in which the child cannot remain safely within the home, Social Services may seek custody and place the child as appropriate. Social Services has a primary responsibility for the protection of the victim(s) and this role continues throughout the casework process.

Social Services makes referrals to appropriate mental health resources for all involved family members. Additionally, Social Services may refer family members to a variety of community resources. The Social Services worker should always assess the need for a medical examination, consulting with police and medical professionals, as deemed appropriate.

2. Law Enforcement Agencies

The role of law enforcement agencies regarding child sexual abuse is to prevent continued victimization and to investigate and refer for criminal prosecution cases of sexual abuse. Police officers should receive specialized training in appropriate methods of dealing with child sexual abuse and should be familiar with this protocol. Both Social Services workers and police must function in a coordinated manner if sexual abuse is to be dealt with adequately.

An allegation of child sexual abuse will be referred to the local law enforcement agency. It may follow an initial Social Services investigation or be a response to a direct report to the police, who will then notify Social Services to coordinate the investigation.

The police investigator and the Social Services worker are both responsible for arranging the investigation to include, for example, joint interviews with the victim, nonoffending spouse, and others as needed.

If the initial report is made to the police, the police response is dictated by the circumstances at the time. In cases where there is immediate danger or threat of violence, the police agency will respond immediately and notify Social Services by telephone. Continued investigation will be coordinated with the assigned Social Services worker.

In situations where the police receive the initial report and do not feel an emergency situation exists, they will promptly contact the local Social Services office and state that they are calling to notify them of a report of child sexual abuse and together, coordinate the investigation. This and all subsequent aspects of the investigation should be closely coordinated between Social Services and the police.

The role of the investigating officer is to determine the status of the victim, establish whether probable cause exists to believe that an offense has occurred, and deal with such issues as jurisdiction of the incident, continuing safety of the victim, evidence, and preparation of a report for the district attorney.

When first reported, medical attention, if needed for the victim, shall be obtained immediately. When in doubt, arrange for medical attention. A criminal investigation will start at this time. It will be the duty of the investigating officer and the Social Services worker to determine if danger exists at this time for the victim and take whatever action is needed to protect the victim, such as removing the victim from the home to a safe location or, if necessary, by court order. This should be done with the basic philosophy in mind that the offender should be the one to leave the house, if at all possible, and that the offender and victim must be separated initially.

In order to take any action, the officer must establish probable cause that a criminal offense has occurred, and will pursue routine police procedures to do so. Cooperation with the agencies, the district attorney, Social Services, mental health professionals, school nurses, and physicians may be necessary to continue the investigation and insure the continued safety of the victim. Evidence will be collected and preserved in accordance with established police procedures. The report is the sum of all the facts which the district attorney must use in making a decision.

3. District Attorney

The district attorney's office has two primary goals in dealing with child sexual abuse cases. The first is the normal prosecutorial function to prosecute the perpetrator. The other important goal is to protect the child.

The parties to the protocol adhere to the belief that, in a system where there is an interagency policy of cooperation, and where adequate treatment is available for the victim, the family, and the offender, the best interests of all concerned dictate prosecution of the offender, whenever it is possible to do so.

In the interests of reaching the best disposition of the case, however, the district attorney's office will seek the recommendation of the Social Services worker and any involved mental health clinician prior to making a decision regarding sentencing. The recommendation of the probation officer is formalized in the form of a Presentence Investigation Report. The presentence report should include an assessment of the offender's amenability to treatment, potential risk to the victim and community, and specialized probation conditions if probation is recommended.

This type of cooperation is essential, particularly if the offender is placed under probation supervision, as there will be a need to structure the supervision with appropriate conditions. Recommendations for release on bail by the district attorney will almost always include a condition that the offender remain out of the home, as well as other conditions designed to protect the victim.

When it is necessary, a juvenile petition may be filed with the family court. In an emergency situation, a child may be taken into custody and placed temporarily in a foster home, or remain in his or her own home though in the custody of Social Services.

If a child is found to be in need of care and supervision either by having a hearing to determine that fact or by a stipulation of the parties, the court has three options. They include:

a. to allow the child to remain with his or her parents or guardian, subject to such conditions and limitations as the court may prescribe, or

b. to place the child under protective supervision, or

c. to transfer legal custody or guardianship to Social Services.

Ultimately, the court will make a determination as to which course of action is in the best interests of the child after receiving input from Social Services, the district attorney, the attorney for the child, the parents, the guardian ad litem for the child, and the parents' attorney.

The prosecution of the perpetrator would be pursued through normal criminal procedures. The end result of such a prosecution could include the imposition by the court of a suspended sentence with conditions of probation, or incarceration. The court normally has input from the defendant, district attorney, and the Probation Department. Factors to be considered in the decision include: the strength of the case, protection of the public, rehabilitation, public education, deterrence, and punishment.

It is important that the office of the district attorney be involved as early as possible once a report is substantiated. It is only through the communication of the parties that the goal of victim protection may be achieved.

4. Medical Aspects of Sexual Abuse

Each hospital in the area should be encouraged to have a protocol regarding treatment of child sexual abuse victims, and staff trained in providing treatment. Agencies involved should, whenever possible, use physicians who are knowledgeable in this special area.

During the medical evaluation—preferably by a physician aware of the special needs of a sexually abused child and also a physician known to the child—the physician attempts to establish evidence of abuse, diagnose and treat trauma and infections secondary to the abuse, and most of all, begins to help the child deal with the psychological trauma caused by the abuse by examining the child in a nonthreatening, gentle, caring manner.

a. It is advisable that children have a medical evaluation. An examination should occur immediately upon discovery if the abuse is recent (within seventy-two hours) or if physical trauma is evident. The exam may be delayed up to a week if the abuse occurred in the past (more than seventy-two hours) and no physical trauma is present. The medical exam should include all history, appropriate tests, physical examination, and recommended treatment.

b. The Social Services worker should help parents understand the need for a physical exam. If the abuse occurred in the distant past and there was no physical harm done to the child, an exam is still useful to assure that no infections/diseases are present.

c. If a parent is vehemently opposed and the child has not been physically harmed, the Social Services worker will have to decide whether the value of the exam outweighs the disruption of a forced exam. In cases where the Social Services worker feels an exam must be done but cannot obtain parental permission, then a court order must be acquired prior to an exam.

5. School/Child Care Center/Pre-school

All school and child care personnel are mandatory reporters of child sexual abuse _____(insert state law)_____. Schools and child care centers should develop their own internal procedures to ensure that this is done and that good communication exists with Social Services. Social Services will provide information and assistance in this regard and will cooperate in establishing and maintaining good working relationships.

School personnel should be aware that it is much easier to deal with such cases, particularly for the child, if Social Services can be involved as early in the day as possible.

6. Mental Health

Local mental health service providers are available for consultation on child sexual abuse cases. For immediate emergency services for therapeutic intervention, call _____ located at _____(insert county address and phone number)_____.

7. Department of Corrections

As the agency with primary responsibility for offender change, Probation/ Parole is still concerned, as its first goal, with protection of the child and any potential victims. Probation/Parole will coordinate its normal functions with the other involved agencies, particularly with the Social Services worker and the mental health clinician treating the offender. Maintaining confidentiality regarding the offender's issues is seen as a block to effective treatment, and information will be shared freely with involved workers to facilitate treatment and protection of the child. A major function of the probation officer is seen as case planning, supervising court-imposed mandates, monitoring, and providing surveillance of the offender as well as working collaboratively with other agencies.

There are a number of situations where the probation officer is involved:

a. At the onset of the case to add additional knowledge of an alleged offender to an ongoing investigation.

b. If the perpetrator is under Probation/Parole supervision at the time of the alleged offense, the supervising officer could have him or her removed from the home immediately. Additional conditions could be modified through a court parole hearing. The supervising officer also can bring a violation of probation or parole and recommend modification of existing conditions or incarceration.

c. Prior to sentencing, the probation officer usually will prepare the presentence report for the sentencing judge with recommendations for disposition. In this situation, the probation officer may rely heavily on the judgments among the professionals involved in the case.

d. If the perpetrator is taking responsibility for the offense and placed on probation supervision, the probation officer is responsible to see that the offender is following the court-mandated treatment program. The probation officer will coordinate activities with Social Services and mental health (victim and offender clinician) to ensure that appropriate decisions are made effecting the victim and family. Under no circumstances will the probation officer allow the offender to return to the home without prior discussion and agreement with the Social Services worker, the nonoffending spouse, child, and the clinicians involved with the offender and family members.

8. Child Sexual Abuse Response (CSAR) Team:

The Sexual Abuse Response Team shall also serve as a consultation and referral team in the treatment of sexual abuse victims and their families. The team approach may be especially helpful in increasing understanding and communication among involved professionals as well as in developing case plans.

9. Adult Correctional Facilities

In the event that an offender is incarcerated, the assigned institutional case manager and parole officer will coordinate release plans closely with the Social Services worker involved with the family. Special conditions of parole may mandate continued involvement in a treatment program, level of contact with the offender's children, or other children, and any other special conditions of parole deemed appropriate by the case managers and approved by the parole board.

III. Implementation and Modification

This protocol shall take effect upon approval of the agencies and individuals involved. Any subsequent changes, additions, or deletions will be submitted to each of the parties to the protocol before being made.

The parties to the protocol recognize that no written document can cover all of the situations that may arise, but are committed to a cooperative effort in this area. Recognizing that problems will occur within and between agencies, the parties to this protocol are committed to a continual effort to improve methods of dealing with child sexual abuse, examining specific problems where they occur, and resolving them in a cooperative manner.

District Attorney	Date		Social Services	Date

Mental Health Agency	Date		Probation and Parole	Date

Child Sexual Abuse Response Team	Date		Law Enforcement	Date

Vermont Assessment of Sex-offender Risk

NAME: LAST	FIRST	MIDDLE	DOB:	AGE:	OFFENSE:

RE-OFFENSE RISK

1. Prior Sex Offense Convictions
none = 0   one = 10 two or more = 20

2. Prior Adult Convictions
(do not count item on #1)
none = 0   one = 1   two or three = 3
four to six = 5   seven or more = 10

**3. VOP's and Other Court Order
Violations During Past Five Years**
none = 0   one = 2   two or more = 5

4. Force Used During Current Offense
hands-off offense = 0   hands-on offense = 5
force greater than necessary to gain compliance or clear
threats of physical harm to victim or others = 8
use of potentially deadly weapon = 10

5. Relationship to Victims
living with at time of offense = 0   nonresidential
relative/acquaintance = 5   stranger = 10

6. Male Victim and/or History of Exhibitionism
none = 0   yes = 10

7. Deviant Sexual Fixation (for hands-off
see instructions)
single victim and history of consenting, age appropriate
sexual relationships = 0   two to four victims and history of
consenting, age appropriate sexual relationships = 5   five
or more victims and/or little or no history of consenting,
age appropriate sexual relationships = 10

8. Alcohol Abuse During Past Five Years
no problems = 0   some legal or social
problems = 3   serious life disruption = 5

9. Drug Abuse During Past Five Years
no problems = 0   some legal or social
problems = 3   serious life disruption = 5

10. Address Changes During Past Year
none = 0   one = 2   two or more = 5

11. Time Employed or in School During Past Year
60% or more = 0   40%-59% = 2   under 40% = 5

**12. Re-offense During or After Treatment, or
Terminated Unsuccessfully from Treatment**
none = 0   yes = 20

13. Amenability to Outpatient Treatment
full or partial admission and willing to participate in
treatment = 0 denies offense or unwilling to participate in
treatment = 10

Total

Copyright 1994
R. J. McGrath & S. E. Hoke
Research Edition
(Reprinted by permission)

VIOLENCE RISK

**1. Prior Convictions for Crimes
Involving Violence**
none = 0   one = 5   two = 10   three = 15   four or more = 20

**2. Prior Conviction for a Crime Involving
a Potentially Deadly Weapon**
none = 0   yes = 15

3. Force Used During Current Offense
hands-off offense = 0   hands-on offense = 5
force greater than necessary to gain compliance or clear
threats of physical harm to victim or others = 15
use of potentially deadly weapon = 30

4. Sexual Intrusiveness of Current Offense
hands-off = 0   fondling = 3   digital penetration,
fellatio, or cunnilingus = 5   actual or attempted penile
penetration of vagina or anus = 10   bizarre or ritualistic
behavior = 20

5. Physical Harm to Current Victim
no medical treatment required = 0   injury not
requiring formal medical attention = 10   treated for injury
and released = 20   hospitalized = 30

**6. Victim Under Age 5, Over Age 55, or
Mentally or Physically Disadvantaged**
no= 0   yes = 10

Total

RISK SCORE

RE-OFFENSE RISK (vertical axis): 10, 20, 30, 40, 50, 60, 70, 80
VIOLENCE RISK (horizontal axis): 10 20 30 40 50 60 70 80
High / Moderate / Low

Aggravating/Mitigating Factors (optional)

RATER:	DATE:

Scoring Instructions

This instrument is a screening tool designed for assessing risk of adult male sex offenders. Although preliminary reliability and validity studies are encouraging, it should still be considered a research tool. The instrument yields a "Re-offense Risk" score and a "Dangerousness Risk" score to achieve an overall "Risk Score." Scores may underestimate or overestimate the actual risk of some offenders. Raters should consider the aggravating and mitigating factors not addressed by the instrument when making placement and supervision decisions. These factors should be noted on the scoring sheet. Most offenders who score in the "Low" range, and many who score in the "Moderate" range, can be safely supervised and treated in a community setting. Offenders who score in the "High" range generally require incarceration to protect the public.

RE-OFFENSE RISK—(If current crime involves multiple victims, score the most serious offense.)

1. Score if the underlying nature of the crime was a sexual offense (e.g., simple assault reduced from sexual assault).
2. "Prior adult convictions" includes DWI's and C&N's, but excludes other motor vehicle convictions.
3. Self-explanatory.
4. Self-explanatory.
5. Self-explanatory.
6. "Exhibitionism" does not include genital exposure that is a prelude to sexual activity with a victim.
7. Because hands-off offenders typically have a larger number of victims than hands-on offenders, consider the hands-off offender's history of consensual sexual relationships when scoring this item. Also, consider the age of the offender and the opportunity that he has had to engage in age-appropriate sexual relationships when scoring this item.
8. Self-explanatory.
9. Self-explanatory.
10. Self-explanatory.
11. Score 0 if offender is retired or disabled.
12. "Treatment" is specialized treatment designed to treat sexual deviancy by a trained professional.
13. "Partial admission" means the offender admits to and accepts at least some responsibility for committing a sexual offense. "Willing to participate in treatment" means that the offender agrees to participate in an approved treatment program. Evaluators may decide to recommend incarceration for offenders who

have a "Low" or "Moderate" "Risk Score" but are not "Amenable to Outpatient Treatment."

VIOLENCE RISK—(If current crime involves multiple victims, score the most serious offense.)

1. Score for prior hands-on sexual offenses. Score if the underlying nature of the crime was violent (e.g., Disturbing the Peace reduced from Simple Assault).
2. Self-explanatory.
3. Self-explanatory.
4. "Bizarre or ritualistic behavior" includes activities such as bondage, urinating or defecating on the victim, and torture.
5. "Injury not requiring formal medical attention" includes minor bruises, scratches, and abrasions for which the victim does not need the attention of trained medical personnel. "Treated for injury and released" includes treatment for a sexually transmitted disease that was transmitted by the offender, but it does not include a medical exam performed solely for obtaining evidence about a sexual assault.
6. "Mentally or Physically Disadvantaged" includes mental illness, mental retardation, severe alcohol or drug intoxication, and any other impairment that seriously compromises the victim's ability to defend him or herself from abuse or provide a credible report about the abuse to authorities.

References

Abel, G., J. Becker, M. Mittelman, J. Cunningham-Rathner, J. Rouleau, and W. Murphy. 1987. Self-reported Sex Crimes of Nonincarcerated Paraphiliacs. *Journal of Interpersonal Violence.* Vol. 2, No. 1. March. 3-25.

Abel, G., M. Mittelman, and J. Becker. 1985. Sexual Offenders: Results of Assessment and Recommendations for Treatment. In M. H. ben-Aron, S. Huckle, and C. Webster, eds. *Clinical Criminology, the Assessment and Rx of Criminal Behavior.* Toronto: M & M Graphic Ltd.

Abney, V., and R. Priest. 1995. African Americans and Sexual Child Abuse. In Lisa Aronson Fontes, ed. *Sexual Abuse in Nine North American Cultures.* Thousand Oaks, California: Sage Publications.

Abrams, S. 1989. Probation Polygraph Surveillance of Child Abusers. *National Prosecutors Association Journal.* Vol. 22.

Abrams, S., and E. Osgood. 1986. Polygraph Surveillance of Probationers. *Polygraph.* 17:174- 218.

Alexander, M. 1993. Sex Offender Treatment: A Response to the Furby *et al.,* Quasi-meta Analysis. A paper presented at the Association for the Treatment of Sexual Abusers 12th Annual Conference, November 10-13, 1993. Boston, Massachusetts.

Allen, C. 1991. *Women and Men Who Sexually Abuse Children: A Comparative Analysis.* Brandon, Vermont: Safer Society Program.

Association for the Treatment of Sexual Abusers. 1993. The ATSA Practitioner's Handbook. Lake Oswego, Oregon: Association for the Treatment of Sexual Abusers.

Becker, J., and E. Coleman. 1988. Incest. In V. Van Hasselt, A. Morrison, and M. Hensen. *Handbook of Family Violence.* New York: Plenum Press.

Comas-Diaz, L. 1995. Puerto Ricans and Sexual Child Abuse. In Lisa Aronson Fontes, ed. *Sexual Abuse in Nine North American Cultures.* Thousand Oaks, California: Sage Publications.

Cornelius, Gary F. 1994. *Stressed Out: Strategies for Living and Working with Stress in Corrections.* Laurel, Maryland: American Correctional Association.

Cross, T., and L. Saxe. 1992. A Critique of the Validity of Polygraph Testing in Child Sexual Abuse Cases. *Journal of Child Sexual Abuse.* Vol. 1(4).

Dwyer, M., and S. Rosser. 1992. Treatment Outcome Research Cross-referencing a Six-Month to Ten-Year Follow-Up Study on Sex Offenders. *Annals of Sex Research*. Vol. 5, No. 2.

Featherman, J. 1995. Jews and Sexual Child Abuse. In Lisa Aronson Fontes, ed. *Sexual Abuse in Nine North American Cultures*. Thousand Oaks, California: Sage Publications.

Finkelhor, D., and S. Araji. 1983. *Explanations of Pedophilia: A Four Factor Model*. Durham, New Hampshire: University of New Hampshire.

Fontes, Lisa., ed. 1995. *Sexual Abuse in Nine North American Cultures*. Thousand Oaks, California: Sage Publications.

Freeman-Longo, R., S. Bird, W. Stevenson, and J. Fiske. 1994. *1994 Nationwide Survey of Treatment Programs and Models*. Brandon, Vermont: The Safer Society Press.

Frisbie, L. 1969. Another Look at Sex Offenders in California. Mental Health Research Monograph (No. 12). Sacramento: State of California, Department of Mental Hygiene.

Furby, L., M. Weinrott, and L. Blackshaw. 1989. Sex Offender Recidivism: A Review. *Psychological Bulletin*. Vol. 105, No. 1. 3-30.

Giarretto, H., A. Giarretto, and S. Sgroi. 1978. Coordinated Community Treatment of Incest. In A. Burgess, N. Groth, L. Holmstrom, and S. Sgroi. *Sexual Assault of Children and Adolescents*. Lexington, Massachusetts: Lexington Books.

Groth, N. 1978. Patterns of Sexual Assault Against Children and Adolescents. In A. Burgess, N. Groth, L. Holmstrom, and S. Sgroi. *Sexual Assault of Children and Adolescents*. Lexington, Massachusetts: Lexington Books.

Groth, N., A. Burgess, and L. Holmstrom. 1977. Rape: Power, Anger and Sexuality. *American Journal of Psychiatry*. 134(11).

Haaven, J., R. Little, and D. Petre-Miller. 1990. *Treating Intellectually Disabled Sex Offenders: A Model Residential Program*. Brandon, Vermont: The Safer Society Press.

Hall, G. 1995. Sexual Offender Recidivism Revisited: A Meta-analysis of Recent Treatment Studies. *Journal of Consulting and Clinical Psychology*. Vol. 63, No. 5. 802-809.

Hazelwood, R. 1995. Analyzing the Rape and Profiling the Offender. In R. Hazelwood and A. Burgess, eds. *Practical Aspects of Rape Investigation: A Multidisciplinary Approach*. New York: CRC Press.

Hindman, J., and L. Hutchens. 1990. The Restitution Model: The Restitution Treatment and Training Program. In James Yokley, ed. *The Use of Victim-Offender Communication in the Treatment of Sexual Abuse: Three Intervention Models*. Brandon, Vermont:The Safer Society Press.

Kafka, M. 1994. Sertraline Pharmacotherapy for Paraphilias and Parapilia-Related Disorders: An Open Trial. *Annals of Clinical Psychiatry.* Vol. 6, No. 3.

Knopp, F. 1984. *Retraining Adult Sex Offenders: Methods and Models.* Brandon, Vermont: The Safer Society Press.

Knopp, F., R. Freeman-Longo, and W. Stevenson. 1992. Nationwide Survey of Juvenile and Adult Sex-offender Treatment Programs and Models. Brandon, Vermont: The Safer Society Press.

Krug, R. 1989. Adult Male Report of Childhood Sexual Abuse by Mother: Case Descriptions, Motivations and Long-term Consequences. *Child Abuse and Neglect.* 13, 111-119.

Lanning, K. 1986. *Child Molesters: A Behavioral Analysis for Law Enforcement Officers Investigating Cases of Child Sexual Exploitation.* Washington, D.C.: National Center for Missing and Exploited Children.

Lykken, D. 1981. *A Tremor in the Blood: Uses and Abuses of the Lie Detector.* New York: McGraw-Hill.

Marlatt, G., and J. Gordon. 1980. Determinants of Relapse: Implications For the Maintenance of Change. In P.O. Davidson and S. M. Davidson, eds. *Behavioral Medicine: Changing Health Lifestyles.* New York: Brunner/Mazel.

Marshall, W. L. , and H. Barbaree. 1988. The Long-term Evaluation of a Behavioral Treatment Program for Child Molesters. *Behavior Research and Therapy.* 26, 499-511.

Marshall, W. L., and W. D. Pithers. 1994. A Reconsideration of Treatment Outcome with Sex Offenders. *Criminal Justice and Behavior.* Vol. 21, No. 1. 10-27.

Matthews, R. 1987. Preliminary Typology of Female Sex Offenders. Minneapolis, Minnesota: PHASE and Genesis II for Women.

McGrath, R. 1990. Assessment of Sexual Aggressors: Practical Clinical Interviewing Strategies. *The Journal of Interpersonal Violence.* December.

McGrath, R. 1991. Sex-Offender Risk Assessment and Disposition Planning: A Review of Empirical and Clinical Findings. *International Journal of Offender Therapy and Comparative Criminology.* 35(4).

McGrath, R. 1992. Five Critical Questions: Assessing Sex Offender Risk. *APPA Perspectives.* 16(3), 6-9.

McGrath, R. 1995. Sex Offender Treatment: Does it Work? *APPA Perspectives.* 9(1).

McGrath, R., and S. Hoke. 1994. Vermont Assessment of Sex Offender Risk. Unpublished Test.

Moritsugu, K. 1990. Inmate Chronological Age Versus Physical Age. In *Long-term Confinement and the Aging Inmate Population.* Washington, D.C.: Federal Bureau of Prisons.

National Council of Juvenile and Family Court Judges. 1993. The Revised Report From the National Task Force on Juvenile Sexual Offending, 1993 of the National Adolescent Perpetrator Network. *Juvenile & Family Court Journal.* Vol. 44, No. 4.

National Institute of Corrections. 1986. *Elderly Inmates.* Washington, D.C.: Department of Justice.

O'Connell, M., E. Leberg, and C. Donaldson. 1990. *Working with Sex Offenders.* London: Sage.

Okamura, A., P. Heras, and L. Wong-Kerberg. 1995. Asian, Pacific Island, and Filipino Americans and Sexual Child Abuse. In Lisa Aronson Fontes, ed. *Sexual Abuse in Nine North American Cultures.* Thousand Oaks, California: Sage Publications.

Philips, W. 1996. Culturally Competent Practice Understanding Asian Family Values. The Roundtable. *Journal of the National Resource Center for Special Needs Adoption.* Vol. 10, No. 1.

Pithers, W., L. Beal, J. Armstrong, and J. Petty. 1989. Identification of Risk Factors Through Clinical Interviews and Analysis of Records. In Richard Laws. *Relapse Prevention with Sex Offenders.* New York: Guilford Press.

Pithers, W., K. Kashima, G. Cumming, L. Beal, and M. Buell. 1988. Relapse Prevention of Sexual Aggression. *Annals of the New York Academy of Sciences.* New York: New York Academy of Sciences.

Pithers, W., and D. R. Laws. 1988. The Penile Plethysmograph. In *A Practitioner's Guide to Treating the Incarcerated Male Sex Offender.* Washington, D.C.: National Institute of Corrections.

Pithers, W., J. Marques, C. Gibat, and G. Marlatt. 1983 . Relapse Prevention with Sexual Aggressives: A Self-control Model of Treatment and Maintenance of Change. In J. G. Greer and I. R. Stuart, eds. *The Sexual Aggressor: Current Perspectives on Treatment.* New York: Van Nostrand Reinhold.

Quinsey, V., G. Harris, M. Rice, and M. Lalumiere. 1993. Assessing Treatment Efficacy in Outcome Studies of Sex Offenders. *Journal of Interpersonal Violence.* Vol. 8, No. 4.

Quinsey, V., M. Lalumiere, M. Rice, and G. Harris. 1995. Predicting Sexual Offenses. In Jacquelyn Campbell, IVPS, ed. *Assessing Dangerousness: Violence by Sexual Offenders, Batterers, and Child Abusers.* Thousand Oaks, California: Sage Publications.

Raskin, D. 1986. The Polygraph in 1986: Scientific, Professional and Legal Issues Surrounding Application and Acceptance of Polygraph Evidence. *Utah Law Review.* 1, 29-74.

Reid, J., and F. Inbau. 1977. *Truth and Deception: The Polygraph Technique, 3rd. ed.* Baltimore: Williams & Wilkins.

Resnick, P. 1988. Testifying in Court. Workshop presented in Burlington, Vermont.

Salter, A.1988. *Treating Child Sex Offenders and Victims*. Newbury Park, California: Sage Publications.

Samenow, S. E. 1984. *Inside the Criminal Mind*. New York: Times Books.

Saxe, L., D. Dougherty, and T. Cross. 1985. The Validity of Polygraph Testing: Scientific Analysis and Public Controversy. *American Psychologist*. 40, 355-366.

Schwartz, B. 1988. *A Practitioner's Guide to Treating the Incarcerated Male Sex Offender*. Washington, D.C.: National Institute of Corrections.

Schwartz, B., and H. Cellini. 1995. *The Sex Offender: Corrections, Treatment and Legal Practice*. Kingston, New Jersey: Civic Research Institute, Inc.

Scully, M, T. Kuoch, and R. Miller. 1995. Cambodians and Sexual Child Abuse. In Lisa Aronson Fontes, ed. *Sexual Abuse in Nine North American Cultures*. Thousand Oaks, California: Sage Publications.

Sgroi, S. 1989. Evaluation and Treatment of Sexual Offense Behavior in Persons with Mental Retardation. In *Vulnerable Populations*. Lexington, Massachusetts: Lexington Books.

Stermac, L., A. Davidson, and M. Sheridan. 1995. Incidence of Nonsexual Violence in Incest Offenders. *International Journal of Offender Therapy and Comparative Criminology*. Vol. 39, No. 2. Summer.

Vermont Network of Sex Offender Therapists. 1995. *Practice Guidelines for the Assessment and Treatment of Sex Offenders*, edited by Robert McGrath. Waterbury, Vermont: Vermont Department of Corrections.

Warren, J., R. Reboussin, R. Hazelwood, and J. Wright 1991. Predicting of Rapist Type and Violence from Verbal, Physical, and Sexual Scales. *Journal of Interpersonal Violence*. Vol. 6, No. 1.

United States Department of Justice. 1985. *The Crime of Rape*. Washington, D.C.: United States Department of Justice.

Yochelson, S., and S. Samenow. 1977. *The Criminal Personality: Vol II. The Change Process*. New York: Aronson.

Young, W. 1988. Structuring a Response to Child Sexual Abuse. In A. Salter. *Treating Child Sex Offenders and Victims*. Newbury Park, California: Sage Publications.

Index